# PERSUADING THE PEOPLE

The day will dawn . . .

London: HMSO

Researched and prepared by Publishing Services,
Central Office of Information.
Text by Anthony Osley.

ISBN 0 11 701885 6

HMSO publications are available from:

**HMSO Publications Centre**
(Mail, fax and telephone orders only)
PO Box 276, London SW8 5DT
Telephone orders 0171-873 9090
General enquiries 0171-873 0011
(queuing system in operation for both numbers)
Fax orders 0171-873 8200

**HMSO Bookshops**
49 High Holborn, London WC1V 6HB
(counter service only)
0171-873 0011 Fax 0171-831 1326

68–69 Bull Street, Birmingham B4 6AD
0121-236 9696 Fax 0121-236 9699

33 Wine Street, Bristol BS1 2BQ
0117-9264306 Fax 0117 9294515

9–21 Princess Street, Manchester M60 8AS
0161-834 7201 Fax 0161-833 0634

16 Arthur Street, Belfast BT1 4GD
01232 238451 Fax 01232 235401

71 Lothian Road, Edingburgh EH3 9AZ
0131-228 4181 Fax 0131-229 2734

**HMSO's Accredited Agents**
(see Yellow Pages)
and through good booksellers

# Contents

# Acknowledgments

We would like to thank the staff at the Public Record Office for their assistance and co-operation in making available numerous Ministry of Information files – and of course for their custodianship of 'our' files over the past 50 years and more!

The Imperial War Museum kindly loaned us transparencies of posters by Abram Games and Frank Newbould, and the Imperial War Museum Library provided valuable help, as did the Brighton Central Library.

We are grateful to Abram Games and Edwin Embleton for sparing the time to talk to us about their recollections of their personal involvement in government publicity.

We would also like to acknowledge the Mass Observation Archive as a source of valuable information. Publications consulted in the preparation of this book have been listed on pp. 91–2.

The extract from *The History of Broadcasting in the UK*, Vol III (1970), by Asa Briggs, is reproduced by permission of Oxford University Press.

# Chronology

## 1938

**March:** Germany takes over Austria.

**September:** Munich Agreement signed, providing for the transfer of Sudeten German areas of Czechoslovakia to Germany.

## 1939

**March:** Hitler tears up Munich Agreement by occupying the rest of Czechoslovakia. Britain and France guarantee Poland.

**April:** Military service introduced in Britain, enabling men between 18 and 41 to be called up.

**August:** Signature of the Hitler–Stalin Pact.

**September:** Germany invades Poland. Britain and France declare war on Germany.

## 1940

**January:**  Food rationing introduced in Britain.

**March–April:** German forces invade Norway and Denmark. British and French armies in Norway evacuated.

**May:** Chamberlain resigns. Churchill becomes Prime Minister as head of Coalition Government. Home Guard formed in Britain.

**May–June:** Germany invades and occupies the Low Countries. France defeated by Germany. Britain evacuates its forces from Dunkirk. Fascist Italy enters the war on the side of Germany.

**July–October:** German airforce defeated in the Battle of Britain.

**September:** German Blitz on London begins.

**December 1940–January 1941:** British victory over the Italian army in Libya.

## 1941

**March:** Britain sends troops to Greece. Rommel's Afrikacorps lands in North Africa.

**April:** Germany attacks and occupies Yugoslavia and Greece. British Expeditionary Force evacuated from Greece.

**May:** Allies lose the battle for Crete, which is occupied by Germany.

**June:** Germany invades the Soviet Union. Clothes rationing introduced in Britain.

**August:** Churchill and Roosevelt sign the Atlantic Charter.

**December:** Japan attacks Pearl Harbour and the United States declares war on Japan. USA enters war against Germany and Italy. Conscription extended to women in Britain.

# 1942

**January–February:** Heavy British defeat in Malaya and Singapore at the hands of the Japanese.

**May:** United States defeats Japanese at the naval Battle of Midway.

**October:** British victory at El Alamein over the Afrikacorps.

**November:** US forces land in North Africa.

**December:** Sir William Beveridge's *Report on Social Security* published.

# 1943

**February:** German forces defeated by the Soviet army at Stalingrad. Heaviest air-raids on London since 1941.

**July–August:** Allied invasion of Sicily.

**September:** Allied landings in southern Italy. Italy surrenders.

# 1944

**January:** Soviet army ends siege of Leningrad.

**June:** British and US forces land in Normandy. Rome liberated by the Allies. First flying bomb dropped on London.

**July:** Unsuccessful attempt by German officers on Hitler's life.

**August:** US forces open up new front by invading southern France. Victory for Allies in Normandy.

**September:** Brussels freed.

**October:** Allies held up by defeat at Arnhem. First V-2 rockets land on London.

**December 1944–January 1945.** German Ardennes offensive defeated.

# 1945

**January:** Soviet Army reaches the river Oder, 50 miles from Berlin.

**March:** British and US forces arrive on the Rhine's west bank.

**April–May:** Soviet armies win the battle for Berlin. Hitler commits suicide. British, US and Soviet armies meet at the River Elbe. Allied forces liberate concentration camps at Belsen, Buchenwald and Dachau. Unconditional surrender by German forces. VE Day (8 May).

**July:** Clement Attlee forms Labour government.

**August:** USA drops atomic bombs on Hiroshima and Nagasaki. Japan surrenders. V-J Day (16 August). End of war.

# Introduction

'Careless Talk Costs Lives, Is Your Journey Really Necessary? Coughs and Sneezes Spread Diseases' – all these slogans and more are etched on the memories of people who lived in Britain during the Second World War. They were highly visible – and effective – campaigns.

Add to these the films of the period. If your rations were low, your house cold and your clothes in holes, the cinema was a cheap place to escape to, to be reassured and enthralled by pictures such as *Target for Tonight* and *Fires Were Started*. On the radio Charles Hill, the radio doctor, provided comfort and guidance on everything from breastfeeding to austerity salads.

Beyond these well known manifestations of government publicity in wartime, there was a mass of publications of all kinds: inspirational stickers depicting Monty and Winnie, respectful booklets detailing the dutiful activities of their royal majesties and highnesses, dry reference booklets marshalling the impressive statistics of Britain's war effort – to name but a few. The intended audiences for these messages were equally diverse, among them hard-pressed homemakers struggling to find more clever ways with turnips; Allied seamen on shore leave; and our brothers and sisters in the colonies, tapping rubber, mining bauxite and picking cotton for all they were worth to assist in fighting the good fight.

These publications suggest that the average home-front Briton then is very different from the modern equivalent – if indeed there is one. In his article on D-Day in the *Independent on Sunday* (5.6.94) Neal Ascherson commented on 'a cult of mass discretion observed by the British people'. Without it the absolute secrecy vital to the success of the D-Day landings could not have been maintained. That we were able to be so discreet rests, he believes, 'on a phenomenal lack of self-importance among ordinary British people'. These people were, of course, the same ones who not so long before had had the events leading up to the Abdication so successfully screened from them by the British press. Yet now we demand the truth, however trivial, from the newspapers, and as for Government information . . .

Another element that may come as something of a surprise to readers is the crudeness of some of the specifically anti-Nazi material – for example, *The Battle for Civilisation*. Fifty years without the threat of invasion leaves us with little perception of how an aggressor might be portrayed today. Would similar items have to be subtler today? Perhaps we would see a divergence between the offensive xenophobia of the tabloids and a polite combination of statistical largesse and political correctness in official publications.

Contrasting with the sledgehammer approach is the humour in booklets such as *Nazi German in 22 Lessons*, and some of the postcards depicting reversals of the war in Britain's favour: it is defiant, cheeky, and even lighthearted. Cartoons prove extremely versatile for debunking the enemy, disguising the menace in the anti-gossip message and reconciling the would-be gourmet to yet another potato dish.

*Persuading the People* looks at the background to the government's wartime publicity effort, and describes some of the campaigns and public reaction to them. It is beyond the scope of this publication to provide an exhaustive survey of government publicity from the Second World War, but the many extracts, film stills and reproductions in this book demonstrate in how many different spheres the government sought to influence people, and, reflected back from these materials, is the image of who these people were.

# The wartime publicity machine

The growth of tension in Europe and the gradual destruction of the 1919 Versailles peace settlement by Nazi Germany during the 1930s coincided with massive strides in the development of the mass media. Whereas in the First World War the main publicity vehicles were the written word, the poster and silent films, by the outbreak of war in 1939 radio had become widely available in Britain and Germany. In addition sound film, dating from the late 1920s and used in newsreels, was a potent new means of publicity for politicians, since the millions of regular cinema goers were now able to see and hear them in action. The 1930s also saw the development of British tabloid journalism, exemplified in the brash new tones of papers like the *Daily Mirror*.

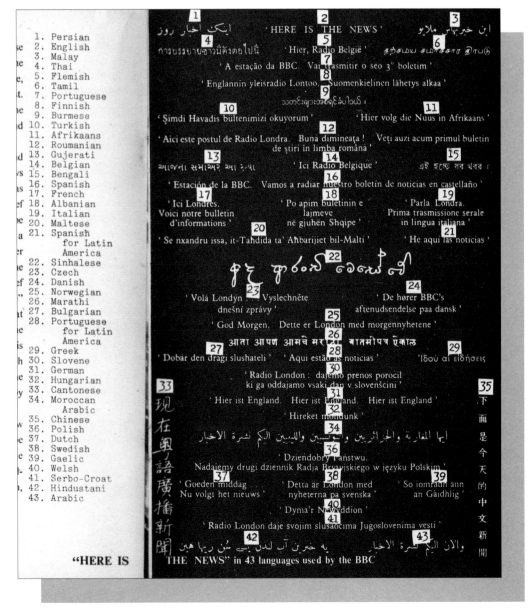

From *London Calling the World* (1945), a booklet in the 'Britain Advances' series that gave a vivid account of how the BBC put together its news broadcasts.

During the 1930s the British Government was faced with two challenges – the territorial expansion of Nazi Germany and that country's head start in propaganda. When Hitler was appointed Chancellor in 1933, immediate steps were taken to establish Nazi control over the media. A new Ministry of Propaganda was created under Joseph Goebbels, the press and cultural organisations becoming subject to its directives. Goebbels encouraged the manufacture of cheap sets – the People's Receiver – which could only receive programmes made and broadcast in Germany, and by 1939 most Germans had a radio set in their homes. Coupled with this, technically well-made newsreels conveyed the Nazi message to millions of cinema fans. Resources were also pumped into propaganda broadcasting for German minority populations in neighbouring countries and for the world as a whole.

In a bid to counter Germany's efforts and those of other dictatorships, the British Council was formed in 1934 to improve cultural relations between Britain and other countries, and four years later the BBC began overseas broadcasting, the number of languages used soaring during the war years, when the BBC's reputation for fair and factual news presentation for overseas audiences was firmly established.

## Forming the Ministry of Information

As Nazi Germany's aggressive foreign policy became increasingly evident in the mid 1930s, the British government made plans to create a Ministry of Information in the event of war. It was not the first time: a similar Ministry had been created to boost home front morale during the First World War and had been wound up after victory was achieved.

Mistrust of MOI in a cartoon from the *Western Mail and South Wales News* for 30 August 1940.

A SECRET WEAPON?

There was some opposition to the idea of co-ordinating government publicity efforts; in a minute sent to Prime Minister Neville Chamberlain in June 1938, his chief adviser, Horace Wilson, complained that propaganda by governments had poisoned the international atmosphere and was not a good substitute for getting on with government business, which included devising a rational foreign policy.

This lack of political enthusiasm ensured that when the Ministry of Information (MOI) was formally created in September 1939 there was no clear idea of its functions. Moreover, its top staff were largely academics and civil servants with little direct experience of the media and how it operated. As a result the Ministry became the butt of satirists in its first few months of existence, the comedian Tommy Handley calling it the Ministry of Aggravation. It was also mocked for overstaffing by the *Daily Mirror's* caustic columnist, Cassandra, and other journalists.

The Ministry's operations were also handicapped by bureaucratic infighting between ministers and officials, including departmental press offices who wanted to remain responsible for their own publicity. This was particularly true of the three armed services, who sought to control and censor their own news. Harold Nicolson, then a Ministry junior minister, expressed his concerns in his diary on 3 August 1940:

> 'I am feeling very depressed by the attacks on the Ministry of Information . . . Since the M. of I. should be an offensive instrument, its value to our war-effort will be diminished by this constant sniping from the rear. I well know that much of the Press campaign is selfish, conceited and unfair. But there does remain a grain of truth at the bottom of it. The Ministry is ill-organised and mistakes are made. A Ministry of this character cannot really be conducted efficiently if the majority of the Press are out to sabotage it.'

Suggestions for disseminating propaganda at grass roots level in a minute to Lord Davidson, Controller of Production at MOI.

Reference...........

7/6/40.

To: Lord Davidson

From: Mr. John Rodgers

In addition to the groups which are listed in our memorandum which ought to be used for the dissemination of propaganda on the Home Front, I feel we ought to include postmen and milk roundsmen.

With regard to postmen, I take it the way to approach this would be for us to write a letter to the head civil servant of the G.P.O., asking him if he would circularise all his postmen telling them that they are in a position of trust and they should not repeat idle rumours but they should make sure that they are only expressing the viewpoint which they hear in the B.B.C. bulletins. Could we not do this immediately ?

With regard to the milk roundsmen, I gather that the Express Dairy and United Dairies have already been approached and that their roundsmen have acted as disseminators, leaving copies of leaflets with each bottle of milk. Owing to paper shortage, I feel we ought to concentrate on the milk roundsman himself and get him fully instructed so that he can pass on the correct message by word of mouth.

John Rodgers,
6. 6. 40.

In addition, there were no fewer than three Ministers of Information in the period between September 1939 and July 1941. Stability was finally achieved with the appointment of Brendan Bracken as Minister in July 1941; he lasted until May 1945. Bracken was a close friend of the Prime Minister, Winston Churchill, and his experience of the newspaper industry and its requirements brought major improvements to the Ministry's operations. There was also a similar turnover in the number of the Ministry's Directors General, three serving between November 1939 and December 1941. Continuity was eventually established with Sir Cyril Radcliffe, who remained in office from December 1941 to the end of the war.

The objectives of the Ministry, as defined by the War Cabinet in July 1941, were:

> 'to publicise and interpret Government policy in relation to the war, to help sustain public morale and to stimulate the war effort, and to maintain a steady flow of facts and opinions calculated to further the policy of the Government in the prosecution of the war.'

Although physically ready with its headquarters, regional information offices and local information committees, the Ministry initially had no co-ordinated system of intelligence on what the public was actually feeling about the course of the war and its impact on them. A disturbing gap between government and governed became apparent, exemplified in one of the first posters – 'Your courage, Your cheerfulness, Your resolution will bring us victory' – which was widely criticised by the press for its patronising tone.

At the end of January 1940 the Ministry acted by setting up its Home Intelligence Division. In addition, it started a programme of wartime social surveys, the investigators being labelled by some sections of the media as 'Cooper's Snoopers', after Duff Cooper, Minister of Information between May 1940 and July 1941.

## Home Intelligence Reports

Home intelligence reports for use by ministers and top officials were compiled by the Home Intelligence Division every week between 1940 and 1944. When victory became certain at the end of 1944, the reports were discontinued.

The purpose of the reports, drawn up on the basis of weekly submissions submitted to Ministry headquarters by home intelligence officers in the 13 regional offices, was to help guide the Ministry in its work by presenting 'an unbiased and objective picture of the state of British public opinion on matters connected with the war' and to assess 'as accurately as possible, the general state of public confidence'.

Regional home intelligence officers collected a lot of raw material in the course of their work since their duties brought them in close contact with the public. Officers cross-checked their sources with others and statements were not considered unless they were backed up by evidence. After vetting by the regional information officer, the reports were then sent to Ministry headquarters in London by express train. Reports were kept secret and were for the sole use of British ministers and their officials.

L O N D O N.

Lack of sleep beginning to tell on people in all districts, showing itself in paleness and lassitude of children and irritability of grown-ups. This is particularly true of poorer quarters where crowded conditions prevail and public shelters are packed and noisy at night. Unhygienic and insanitary conditions reported in large buildings used as shelters in Bethnal Green, City etc. where hundreds of people of mixed ages and sexes congregate with bedding and remain all night. Shelters not designed for mass sleeping, and responsible people fear serious consequences of impaired health and possible epidemics. School on Housing Estate in South East London has few attendances because of broken nights and head teacher states that children who come are heavy eyed and white. On some Estates, shelter marshals run public shelters and organise community singing and games of darts in public spirited manner successfully murdering sleep.

Home Intelligence.
31st August, 1940.

A Home Intelligence report on the hardships – some of them not directly attributable to the Germans – of life during the Blitz.

Special training was given to the intelligence officers in order to impress on them the need to 'become impartial recording and assessing machines free from political or other bias'. The basis of the officer's work was a panel of voluntary contacts scattered throughout the region, examples including doctors, priests, shopkeepers, trade union officials, businesspeople and staff from organisations like the Women's Voluntary Service and the Citizens Advice Bureaux. Each region had between 200 and 400 contacts, a proportion of whom were asked every week to submit reports about particular difficulties faced by the public and about any substantial volume of praise or criticism on issues such as rationing. The Ministry took special care to assure its contacts that it was not concerned with snooping on people but with what was said and thought about the war. The regional reports sent to headquarters generally showed a 'high degree of agreement' and uniform trends in the development of public opinion.

Information also came from the network of local information committees, which included representatives of the political parties, local authorities, voluntary bodies and other organisations. The Ministry, however, treated their views with some suspicion on the grounds that the views of one member could colour those of others and that a majority opinion could be recorded instead of a statement of differences. Nevertheless, it recognised that the committees could make a contribution by commenting on public feeling about issues such as shortages of certain commodities in wartime.

Other useful sources of information were the weekly regional reports made by the Ministry's Postal Censorship Division of letters leaving the country, and the reports on home opinion drawn up by chief police officers, which were passed to the Ministry with the agreement of the Home Office.

Information provided by the BBC's Listener Research Department recorded the reaction of the public to news and other programmes broadcast by the Corporation. The Ministry also had access to survey information from public opinion polls undertaken by the Gallup organisation and the British Institute of Public Opinion. Data from the Mass Observation organisation, founded in 1937, was also used. Mass Observation was a fact-finding body with a team of trained investigators and a nationwide panel of voluntary observers who sent in reports on the social behaviour and views of groups of people and individuals.

The weekly reporting system did not go unchallenged. On 4 April 1942, the Prime Minister, Winston Churchill, wrote a personal minute to Brendan Bracken commenting that 'there is hardly anything in this which could not have been written by a man sitting in a London office and imagining the echoes in the country to the London Press'. Churchill added: 'I doubt very much whether this survey is worth its trouble. How many people are engaged upon it, and how much does it cost?'

Responding on 13 April, Bracken defended the efforts of his staff, pointing out that

> '. . . there is really no doubt that the final summary report does in fact proceed from the genuine collection of views and opinions from a large number of independent non-official people all over the country. It is not, and does not pretend to be, an accurate survey of the total opinion in the country, but it is looked upon as providing useful pointers to trends of feeling.'

Bracken's reply evidently convinced Churchill that the Home Intelligence reports should continue, since no further criticism of weekly report came from the Prime Minister.

## The Government and the BBC

When war broke out there were over 9 million radio licence holders. This large potential audience inevitably affected the Government's relations with the BBC at a time of national emergency.

In 1939 Government powers over the BBC were transferred from the Postmaster General to the Ministry of Information. These concerned issues such as programme matters, hours of broadcasting and the possible control of radio services in an emergency. Neville Chamberlain assured the House of Commons that the Ministry had 'no desire and, indeed, no power to interfere with the discretion of the Corporation in their choice of entertainment programmes'. In 1940 the licence payment was replaced by a grant for the BBC from the Government.

Shortly after taking over as Prime Minister in May 1940, Churchill requested from the Minister of Information 'some proposals from you for establishing a more effective control over the BBC'. The Minister, Duff Cooper, sent a memorandum on 20 May pointing out that 'the BBC have accepted hitherto and will continue to accept general guidance from the Ministry and will bend to our decisions after having made their observations.' Cooper added that the BBC had agreed that no political broadcasts would be arranged 'without my approval'. He also urged Government ministers to make full use of the radio as a publicity vehicle.

Frank Newbould was an assistant designer at the War Office. Britain as a sunny arcadia was a recurring theme in much official propaganda.

General Montgomery, Commander-in-Chief of the British Eighth Army, which has so distinguished itself in the North African campaign, and in the Allied offensive in Southern Europe.

LE GENERAL DE GAULLE

Pour la liberté

G.P.D. 445/2/5

Safe in their hands? Postcards and stickers promoting the image of these Allied luminaries.

THE RT. HON. WINSTON S. CHURCHILL

*With every good wish Christmas 1944*

For Freedom

LE MARECHAL STALINE

Pour la liberté

G.P.D. 445/2/5

The booklet *No!* contrasted life under Nazi rule with a bucolic, peaceful Britain. Elsewhere its fuzzy photographs of Nazi atrocities back up exhortations to resist surrender to the enemy.

# NO!

The final victory of the forces of Freedom will ensure that the Nazi dream of a slave world shall never come to pass

IT SHALL NOT HAPPEN HERE · ·
BRITAIN

THE ancient cradle of mankind's freedom has only maintained the liberties of her peoples by ceaseless vigilance, and by being ever ready to fight for them, to the death, against the tyrant's threat. Liberty so hard-won and so hardly kept shall never be lost by Britain through complacence and lethargy. ALL Britons will rally to that call—crying with a united voice IT SHALL NOT HAPPEN HERE!

A village church in Devon, surrounded by fruitful fields and backed by wide moorlands which have never acknow-ledged a usurper's rule—symbols of Britain's ancient, progressive culture.

Flying fantasy: an unsigned picture in the 'War in Pictures' series

# THE RIGHTS OF BRITISH CITIZENS

**FREEDOM OF SPEECH,** or the right of any man to say what he will, subject to the law which punishes slander—the abuse of that right.

**FREEDOM OF PERSON AND MOVEMENT,** or the right to act freely within the bounds of the law, and to have a fair trial in a court of law if one is charged with going outside the bounds.

47

*Great Britain To-day and To-morrow* extolled the virtues of Britain past and present. Northern Ireland is included, even though it was left out of the title.

*I*N this war the British regard victory—symbolised by the traditional laurel branch —not merely as a military achievement, but as an opportunity to create conditions in which will be possible a greater measure of well-being, happiness and security in human life.

This opportunity—the fruit of long effort and endurance—will not be lightly valued, nor will it be carelessly used. The problems of social reconstruction, extraordinarily complex under today's conditions, have for some time been the subject not only of widespread popular discussion, but of specialised and detailed planning.

Great Britain is determined that out of the misery and destruction of war shall come a new era of human happiness. In the following pages some indication is given of the new Great Britain—essentially the same in spirit, though ruthlessly changed where necessary—which will rise from the ashes of the present conflict.

In the closing stages of hostilities the brave new post-war world was set out tantalisingly in a number of publications.

Although the Government had such final authority over the BBC through the Ministry of Information, it decided in effect not to exercise it, particularly under the Bracken regime. The fact that there was a coalition government between May 1940 and 1945 helped minimise possible rows between the Government and the BBC over internal British political controversies. Bracken summed up the general position in a speech made in December 1943:

> 'At the beginning of this war the Government were given power to interfere in the affairs of every institution in this country including the BBC. And though I am always willing to take responsibility for all the BBC's doings, I have refused to interfere in the policies of the Corporation. The Governors and many members of the staff often consult with the Ministry of Information and sometimes they condescend to ask us for our advice and we give it for what it is worth. But I can say from my own personal experience that no attempt has ever been made by the Government to influence the news-giving or any other programme of the BBC. In fact, I am constantly advising my friends in the BBC of the desirability of being independent and of being very tough with anyone who attempts to put pressure upon you.' (quoted in *The History of Broadcasting in the UK*, Vol III, by Asa Briggs).

Briggs concluded that the BBC 'retained throughout the war a very substantial measure of independence'.

Churchill himself made full use of radio as a publicity vehicle. *(London Calling the World)*

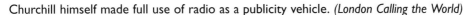

Mr. Churchill at the microphone

*Facing page:* A watercolour by the distinguished artist Dame Laura Knight, commissioned – not without some intense negotiation – to publicise the Women's Land Army.

# The Press in Wartime

The press, too, enjoyed considerable freedom during the Second World War, since censorship was maintained on a voluntary basis. Under the system newspapers were invited to submit to the Ministry of Information Censorship Division reports that might contain information of value to the enemy. Defence Notices were produced, giving examples of the items which would not be passed by the Censorship Division and those on which an opinion by Censorship would be desirable; in turn the newspapers voluntarily agreed to accept advice from Censorship on these issues. This voluntary system was backed by legal sanctions in the form of the Defence Regulations, under which it was an offence for anyone to publish or convey to the enemy information that could assist him in carrying on the war. Under this power the Government had to give the newspaper concerned a warning; if this was disregarded a prosecution could follow. Another Defence Regulation allowed the Government to suppress a newspaper if it was fomenting opposition to the war and it was under this provision that the Communist *Daily Worker* was closed down in January 1941, when the Hitler–Stalin Pact was still in operation.

During Bracken's reign as Minister, he made clear to the House of Commons his belief in free speech and his opposition to the idea of censors editing newspapers. Moreover, it was clearly established that there should be no censorship of opinion, the result being periods of lively controversy in the press about Government policies.

In October 1941 the *Sunday Pictorial* caustically attacked the composition of the Government, telling Churchill to give half his ministers a permanent rest cure. Although Churchill demanded the *Pictorial's* suppression, Home Secretary Herbert Morrison successfully advised the War Cabinet that the 'democratic principle of freedom for expression of opinion means taking the risk that harmful opinions may be propagated'. On another occasion Churchill, angered by criticisms printed in the *Daily Mirror* in 1942, complained to one of its directors that 'there is a spirit of hatred and malice against the Government which is after all not a Party but a National Government . . .'.
After the publication of a controversial Zec cartoon, the *Mirror* editor was carpeted in 1942 by Morrison, who threatened the paper with suppression.

Although press criticism did annoy government ministers, co-operation also took place. The magazine *Picture Post*, with its readership of 5 million to satisfy, was prepared to collaborate with the Ministry of Information on the production of issues devoted to special topics such as the United States or the Battle of the River Plate, the Ministry providing the extra paper required. In addition, publishers were on occasion willing to work with the Ministry; Oxford University Press, for instance, published two books about Germany which were prepared by the Ministry.

EXAMPLES OF ARTICLES PUBLISHED IN THE PRESS WHILE THE
SUBJECT MATTER WAS STOPPED IN CENSORSHIP.    THIS LIST
IS BY NO MEANS EXHAUSTIVE AND ONLY COVERS THE LAST 14
                        DAYS.

| STORY | NEWSPAPER |
|---|---|
| Mentioning of H.M.S. "Cumberland" outside Montevideo. | Daily Sketch, Daily Herald, Daily Express, Sunday Graphic, Daily Mail, Daily Telegraph, Evening Standard. |
| Mentioning of "Barham" outside Montevideo. | Several Newspapers. |
| H.M.S. "Exeter" proceeding to Bahia Blanca. | Daily Telegraph, News Chronicle & others. |
| H.M.S. "Exeter" (100 casualties). | Daily Telegraph, Associated Press, (i.e. all Provincial Press). |
| Sinking of the "Fire King". | Daily Mirror. |
| Sinking of I.W. "Winck". | Daily Telegraph & others. |
| Sinking of "Dinard" | Daily Telegraph. |
| Grounding of "Louis Scheid". | Daily Telegraph. |
| Tanker torpedoed. | Daily Express. |
| Sinking of U-boat. | Daily Express. |
| Mention of "Leipzig". | Evening News & others. |
| U-boat captured. | Daily Express. |
| Polish Submarine escapes. | News Chronicle. |
| Survivors of "Magnus". | News Chronicle. |

Newspapers sometimes 'jumped the gun'.

# The Ministry and General Morale

Although some civilians in Britain suffered limited casualties from German bombs during the First World War, they were not generally in the front line. Twenty years later it was a different story: mass bombing took place, killing thousands of civilians and injuring many more. Moreover, the needs of modern war required the mass mobilisation of people and the economy to provide fighting forces and the equipment necessary to sustain their efforts. It was, therefore, essential for the Ministry of Information and other government departments, such as the Ministry of Food, to do everything they could to sustain morale.

Following a year of Home Intelligence reports (see p. 10), Stephen Taylor, the head of Home Intelligence, submitted a report on 1 October 1941 indicating that good morale depended on material factors such as adequate food, warmth, rest, a secure base, and safety and security for dependants. Morale was also affected by mental factors, including belief in victory, equality of sacrifice, the justice of the war and efficient leadership. Taylor wrote that personal experience was the most powerful agent in forming public opinion, followed by the radio, which had a 'degree of universality not possessed by any group of newspapers' and was 'regarded as having no axes to grind'. On the enemy, Taylor commented that

> 'particular exception is taken to anything which can possibly be regarded as "kid-glove" handling of our enemies. It is for the absence of "kid-gloves", as well as for many other qualities, that the public admires and respects the leadership of the Prime Minister.'

Back to work in the aftermath of an air raid. *Front Line* recorded the defiance and fortitude of the public in the face of the Blitz, and was well received.

Taylor concluded that the British public was pragmatic, while possessing 'a deep rooted belief in the liberty of the subject' and a sense of fair play. It also had 'a great capacity for righteous indignation when things go wrong' and then blamed the press, the radio and, above all, the Ministry of Information. Nevertheless it 'had a very high degree of common sense' and, given the relevant facts, would 'listen to and accept explanations when it will not accept exhortations'. There was, Taylor noted, 'a new sense of purpose in life with a clear-cut objective in view – winning the war' and 'everyone has some sense of personal participation in the work of the country'. Moreover,

> 'Thanks to dispersal by evacuation, higher wages for the undernourished, rationing for the overnourished, and milk for children, general health has, on the whole, improved rather than deteriorated.'

## Exhortation or Explanation?

The Ministry of Information was faced with the dilemma of deciding whether to exhort the population to take the action desired by the Government or to focus publicity on explaining and backing up government measures. In the first part of the war exhortation took priority and this was not always to the liking of the population, as Home Intelligence recognised in July 1940:

> 'There is evidence that political exhortations and "wireless pep talks" are not being well received. People are asking for more information and above all for positive guidance.'

A Home Intelligence paper written in 1941 noted that 'the attempt

## The German Air Force and British Towns . . .

IN AUGUST 1940, the Luftwaffe began its main assault against Britain. It was originally a daylight offensive, designed to sweep the British fighters from the sky. When this failed, the Luftwaffe remorselessly pounded British towns, making the majority of their raids at night.

The first big attack on London came on September 7th 1940. It killed 430 people and seriously wounded 1,600. London endured continuous bombing for 57 nights (September 7th to November 2nd) and thereafter was heavily bombed at frequent intervals until the last big air raid on May 10th 1941. Coventry, Birmingham, Bristol, Sheffield, Manchester, Portsmouth, Southampton, Liverpool, Plymouth, Glasgow, Hull, Belfast—all were heavily raided.

Up to the end of 1941 over 44,600 civilians had been killed, more than half of whom were women or children, while a further 52,000 had been seriously injured. By October 1943, the figure for fatal casualties had risen to over 50,000 and the seriously injured to over 59,600.

Obviously, the Germans believed that indiscriminate bombing of British towns would so lower civilian morale that Britain would speedily collapse. The actual effect of terror raids was rather to rouse the fighting spirit of the British people to a higher pitch than ever before, while the effects of high civilian casualties were more than countered by the encouraging sight of steadily rising war-production figures.

12

*The City of London burns after the big incendiary attack of December 29th 1940.*

LONDON

The booklet *Aerial Bombardment: The Facts* sought to counteract German claims that British bombing was directed at civilian targets.

to use propaganda as a substitute for legislation is a waste of energy, time and money' and that there was little evidence that exhortatory campaigns had any appreciable effect:

> 'It is in the fields of explanation, interpretation and instruction in wartime citizenship that the most useful scope, as well as the greatest successes, of Government propaganda are found . . .'

In April 1942 Bracken wrote a memo stressing that there

> 'must be more explanation: not only about the armed forces and the war situation but also about production, labour, wartime restrictions and the big problems that affect the life of everyone today . . . We must stop appealing to the public or lecturing at it. One makes it furious, the other resentful'.

As the historian of the Ministry, Ian McLaine, noted:

> 'With the constant and thorough analyses of the Home Intelligence Division as a sure guide, the Ministry also came to regard the British people as sensible and tough, and therefore entitled to be taken into the Government's confidence.'

# Rousing the people against the enemy

No long war can be fought without attempting to rouse the people against the enemy. One of the first Ministry of Information publications – quoting extensively from the relevant diplomatic documents – pointed out that Britain had done its utmost to avoid war and that it was wholly the fault of aggression by Germany's Nazi rulers. This point was also emphasised by Chamberlain's broadcast to the German people on 4 September 1939:

> 'In this war we are not fighting against you, the German people, for whom we have no bitter feelings, but against a tyrannous and forsworn regime which has betrayed not only its own people but the whole of Western civilisation and all that you and we hold dear.'

AN INTERVIEW WITH HITLER.           *(August* 23)

On August 23 Sir Nevile Henderson reported his first interview with Hitler earlier in the day. Hitler was " excitable and un-compromising " ; his language was " violent and exaggerated both as regards England and Poland."

" He began by asserting that the Polish question would have been settled on the most generous terms if it had not been for England's unwarranted support. I drew attention to the inaccuracies of this statement, our guarantee having been given on 31st March and Polish reply on 26th March. He retorted by saying that the latter had been inspired by a British press campaign, which had invented a German threat to Poland the week before. Germany had not moved a man any more than she had done during the similar fallacious press campaign about Czecho-Slovakia on the 20th May last year.

He then violently attacked the Poles, talked of 100,000 German refugees from Poland, excesses against Germans, closing of German institutions and Polish systematic per-secution of German nationals generally. He said that he was receiving hundreds of telegrams daily from his per-secuted compatriots. He would stand it no longer, etc. I interrupted by remarking that while I did not wish to try to deny that persecutions occurred (of Poles also in Germany) the German press accounts were highly exaggerated. He had mentioned the castration of Germans. I happened to be aware of one case. The German in question was a sex-maniac, who had been treated as he deserved. Herr Hitler's retort was that there had not been one case but six.

*How Hitler Made the War* reported the minutiae of the fraught negotiations leading up to the outbreak of war on 3 September 1939.

# Anger Campaign

As the war escalated in the spring of 1940, the Ministry accepted that there should be no separation between the German people and Nazism and decided to launch its 'anger' campaign, drawing the population's attention to the brutality of Nazi rule in order to reinforce its willingness to continue the struggle. Literature about Nazi atrocities and human rights violations formed a staple diet of Ministry leaflets and pamphlets. A publication on Nazi education, for instance, said:

DR. HANS FRANK
Solicitor. Became Hitler's Chief
Legal Adviser. Chief Minister of
Justice, Bavaria, 1933. Appointed
Governor-General of Poland in
1939, he has already been
responsible for the murders of
200,000 Poles and 200,000 Jews.
Until recently he was a member
of the Reich Cabinet.

DR. JOHANNES STARK
Doctor of Physics. Won
Nobel Price for Physics,
1919. Became President of
the Reich Physical-Technical
Institute and German Research
Association in 1933. He rejected
Einstein's Theory on the
grounds that Einstein is
a Jew.

16

These two were among the 'new leaders of Nazi learning', according to the booklet *Education under Nazi Rule*.

'To keep their subjects down, these tyrants must do more than suppress liberty of opinion and access to knowledge in the adult: they must prevent the minds of children from ever opening, and turn the young generation into a dull mass of unthinking, regimented and perverted slaves.'

After the Dunkirk evacuation, a pamphlet, *What Would Happen If Hitler Won?*, said:

'If Hitler won you couldn't make a joke in the pub without being afraid that a spy may not get you run in or beaten up; you could not talk freely in front of your children for fear that they might give you away (in Germany they are encouraged to); if you were a worker you would be at the mercy of your employer about hours and wages, for you would have no trade union.'

A booklet entitled *No!* drew a graphic picture of Nazi tyranny, pointing out: 'The despotic rule of a half-crazed Führer, the fantastic dreams of power with which he had in the past filled so many hysterical pages, became a horrible reality in Germany.' It continued: 'You cannot make terms with the tiger. It is YOU - or HE . . . you must kill him or cage him, before he kills you and yours after the manner of its kind.'

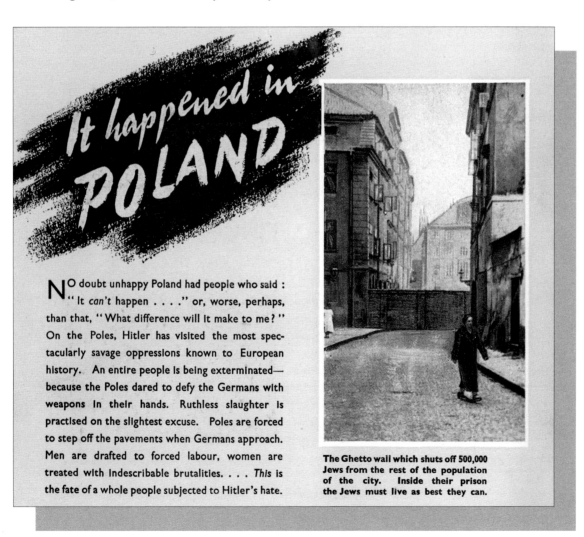

It happened in POLAND

NO doubt unhappy Poland had people who said : "It *can't* happen . . . ." or, worse, perhaps, than that, "What difference will it make to me?" On the Poles, Hitler has visited the most spectacularly savage oppressions known to European history. An entire people is being exterminated—because the Poles dared to defy the Germans with weapons in their hands. Ruthless slaughter is practised on the slightest excuse. Poles are forced to step off the pavements when Germans approach. Men are drafted to forced labour, women are treated with indescribable brutalities. . . . *This* is the fate of a whole people subjected to Hitler's hate.

**The Ghetto wall which shuts off 500,000 Jews from the rest of the population of the city. Inside their prison the Jews must live as best they can.**

From the booklet *No!*

Churchill also set the prevailing tone in his June 1941 broadcast, pledging aid to Russia, when he spoke of

> '. . . the Nazi war machine, with its clanking, heel clicking, dandified Prussian officers, its crafty expert agents fresh from the cowing and tying down of a dozen countries. I see also the dull, drilled, docile, brutish masses of the Hun soldiery plodding on like a swarm of crawling locusts.'

# Friends overseas

Because Britain was the one European country challenging Hitler, London became a haven for people from Nazi-occupied countries determined to fight on. Governments in exile were formed and spoke to their peoples on the radio via the BBC overseas services. Perhaps the most famous of these broadcasts was that made by General de Gaulle on 18 June 1940, in which he called on the French to resist Nazi occupation. Military uniforms from many European countries were seen on the streets, one of the largest contingents of foreign troops coming from Poland.

From a leaflet entitled 'Something to Give'.

# Dominions and Colonies

Members of the British Empire or Commonwealth joined the war by providing troops and equipment. In tribute to this effort, the Ministry of Information organised a publicity campaign in the later half of 1940 to draw the British people's attention to the vital contributions being made by these countries in the common cause. It kicked off with BBC radio programmes about Commonwealth countries, their leaders being given the chance to address the British people and give them information about their countries and their contribution to the war.

These were followed up by press advertisements, the first – headed 'The Greatest Crusade' – stressing:

> 'By fortifying the spirit of liberty, we are building self-reliant nations of free men. We are the Builders at grips with the Destroyers . . . Under a thin disguise of catchwords, the Nazis have started the old futile game of building a slave empire . . . The British Empire is exactly the opposite. There has been nothing like it in the world before; it is a Commonwealth, a family of free nations – linked together by loyalty to one King. It stands for progress; it is the hope of the future.'

One of a series of postcards highlighting the Commonwealth's contribution to the war effort.

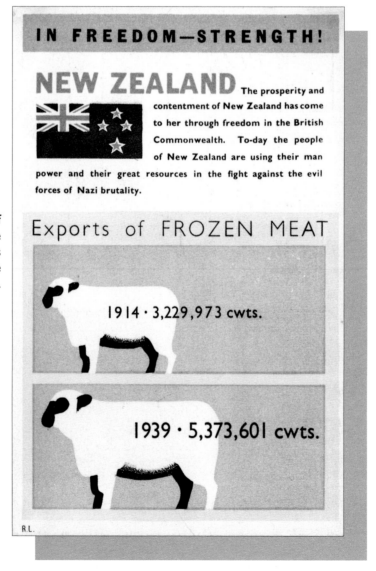

Other advertisements were devoted to the contributions made by individual countries such as India:

> 'DO YOU KNOW THAT INDIA supplies all the jute for making sacks and handbags, that more than half Britain's needs of livestock foods come from India, as well as tea, rice, hides, skins, cotton and manganese? THESE ARE THE SINEWS OF WAR.'

Posters added another boost to the campaign. MIGHTIER YET, one blared, pointing out that the British Empire navies were 'the most powerful seaforce in the world' and that another million tons of British warships were being built.

## The United States

The United States was officially neutral in the first two years of the war. Although facing isolationist sentiment at home, President Franklin Roosevelt made no secret of his support for Britain. He described the US as the arsenal of democracy and supported the British war effort through munitions and other supplies. He and Churchill became close allies, both men signing in August 1941 the Atlantic Charter, which referred to 'the final destruction of Nazi tyranny'. The US entry into the war was precipitated in December 1941 by the Japanese assault on Pearl Harbour and Hitler's misguided declaration of war on the United States.

OIL is the life-blood of mechanised war. The U.S. produces nearly two-thirds of the world's oil. It produces, too, over three-quarters of the world's sulphur, vital to arms production.

TANKS, guns, munitions are flowing from thousands of U.S. factories. Quantity is unlimited, quality is superb. United States machine-power is expanding daily.

United States STEEL industries are huge, modern, efficient. Behind them stand thousands of factories which turn steel into machines. The U.S. makes three out of every four of the world's automobiles.

From 'A Giant Awakes', a leaflet produced to celebrate the United States joining the war.

British official publicity in the United States was issued through the British Library of Information in New York, which was founded in the 1920s. Once the London blitz began, the Ministry of Information realised that the American press and radio correspondents, who were full supporters of the British war effort, could perform a vital role in influencing US opinion through their descriptions of the Luftwaffe's assault on the British capital and of the reactions of a people under siege. The CBS correspondent, Edward Murrow, was allowed to make a broadcast from the roof of Broadcasting House during an air raid; in addition, he was a tireless traveller on the streets in search of a story, observing fire watchers and the civil defence services in action and using radio sound effects for maximum impact on the audience back home.

Britain was the only staging post for an allied invasion to liberate Western Europe from Nazi rule. From early 1942 US soldiers began arriving in Britain in large numbers, bringing with them vast amounts of equipment. By the spring of 1944, southern England in particular was an armed camp as US and British forces prepared for the Normandy landings.

In 1942 a welcome booklet was issued to American soldiers by the British Government:

> 'The people will be very glad to see you, but their enthusiasm is usually of a rather shy sort and you may not be aware, at first, of the warm friendliness they feel towards you.'

The booklet stressed that

> 'the gayer side of British life has been subordinated to the grim business of war . . . the streets are black at night and it is very difficult for a stranger to find his way about. Food is plentiful, up to a point, but there are few luxuries. We have made this island into a fortress . . . '

The booklet warned the newcomers about air raids:

> 'If the sirens go, and you are in the streets, take cover. Quite a few English people have learned that it isn't very smart to stand in the street when the bombs and shrapnel start falling . . . Another thing – don't shine a naked light or a flashlight – it's an offence in this country. If you have a flashlight, cover the bulb with a couple of thicknesses of white tissue paper.'

A special edition of *Picture Post* was put on sale in Britain and the United States in order to promote good relations between British civilians and American troops. In practice relations between the Americans and the British presented no major difficulties since both countries were parliamentary democracies and shared similar values in the fight against Hitler.

# The Soviet Union

The Soviet Union, too, became a British ally when Hitler launched his invasion of Soviet territory in June 1941. Prior to this, the Soviet Union was party to the Hitler–Stalin pact, which had divided Poland and other parts of Eastern Europe into German and Soviet spheres of influence.

## CURRENCY

ONE of our quaint English customs is to make the currency as difficult as possible for everybody, including ourselves. You can take it roughly that five shillings (better known as five bob) are equivalent to a dollar. Watch the half crown and the two shilling piece—they're very similar in size and design, but the half crown is worth 10 cents more. Various wartime measures have been introduced in this country relating to foreign currency, so please don't try to exchange money except through your own officials or a British bank. Here's a rough guide to the values.

| Coin | Slang Name | Metal | Value |
|---|---|---|---|
| Half penny | Copper | copper | 1 cent |
| Penny | | copper | 2 cents |
| Three pence (Threepenny bit) | | silver or twelve-cornered brass | 5 cents |
| Sixpence | Tanner | silver | 10 cents |
| Shilling | Bob | silver | 20 cents |
| Two shilling piece (Florin) | | silver | 40 cents |
| Half crown | Half-dollar | silver | 50 cents |
| Ten shillings | Ten bob | paper (purple) | 2 dollars |
| Pound | Quid | paper (blue & brown) | 4 dollars |

THE enemy has a weakness for printing British paper money which we don't want to encourage, so we don't let any bills in except through certain official channels. It is important therefore for you to remember to get rid of paper money *before* you leave the country. This does not necessarily mean that you must spend it. We suggest you hand back to the Captain of your ship *before* you sail any unspent money and ask him to credit you with the value in U.S. currency. Actually it is forbidden to take British currency out of the country.

8

HALF PENNY

SIXPENCE

ONE PENNY

SHILLING

PENNY

THREE PENCE (Silver)

TWO SHILLING PIECE

THREE PENCE (Brass)

HALF CROWN

9

[This booklet is issued to all American soldiers, sailors, airmen and merchant seamen with the compliments of the British Government.]

*Printed in England by K.H.K. and W.R.R. Wt. 52293. 4/42.*

### THE ENGLISH SOMETIMES HAVE A DIFFERENT WORD FOR IT

| American | English | American | English |
|---|---|---|---|
| APARTMENT | Flat | FENDER (AUTO) | Wing or Mud-guard |
| AUTOMOBILE | Car | | |
| BATHTUB | Bath | GASOLINE | Petrol |
| BISCUIT | Scone (or Teacake) | HIGHBALL | Whisky and Soda or Ginger Ale |
| BOOT | Riding Boot (Wellington) | | |
| | | HUNTING | Shooting |
| HIGH SHOE | Boot | HOOD (AUTO) | Bonnet |
| LOW SHOE | Shoe | SALOON | Pub |
| CANDY | Sweets | UNDERSHIRT | Vest or Singlet |
| COOKIE | Biscuit | UNDERPANTS OR SHORTS | Pants |
| LETTER-BOX | Pillar-box | | |
| WRENCH | Spanner | PANTS | Trousers |
| SPIGOT (OR FAUCET) | Tap | DRUG-STORE | Chemist |
| | | SIDEWALK | Pavement |
| SUSPENDERS | Braces | DEPOT | Station |
| GARTERS | Suspenders | FREIGHT TRAIN | Goods Train |
| WATER-HEATER | Geyser | FREIGHT CAR | Truck |
| WINDOW-SHADE | Blind | TRUCK | Lorry |
| CHECKERS | Draughts | SUBWAY | Tube or Underground |
| ELEVATOR | Lift | | |
| STREET CAR | Tram | | |

Explaining £, s, d to the Americans, and providing a translation, in the *Welcome* booklet (1942).

Within hours of the German invasion, Churchill gave whole-hearted support to the Russians:

> 'No-one has been a more consistent opponent of Communism than I have for the last twenty-five years. I will unsay no word that I have spoken about it. But all this fades away before the spectacle that is now unfolding . . . We are resolved to destroy Hitler and every vestige of the Nazi regime . . . Any man or state who fights on against Nazidom will have our aid . . . It follows therefore that we shall give whatever help we can to Russia and the Russian people. We shall appeal to all our friends and allies in every part of the world to take the same course and pursue it, as we shall, faithfully and steadfastly to the end . . .'

**JANUARY 1942** Hitler's way OUT of Russia! This is an ACTUAL PHOTOGRAPH of some of the vast quantities of Nazi tanks, guns, and armoured vehicles the German A being forced to abandon in its retreat before the powerful Russian offensive.

A fold-out card highlighting success on the Russian front.

The issues of Russia and Communism presented a challenge to the Government's publicists. In August 1941 Ministry of Information officials agreed on the main aims of publicity regarding these issues. These were to promote publicity for Anglo-Soviet co-operation while cold-shouldering co-operation with the British Communist Party or its pro-Soviet organisations. It was happy to work with the Soviet Embassy by organising touring exhibitions about aspects of the Soviet Union and its war effort and promoting factory showings of a film, *USSR at War*.

The stiffness of Russian resistance and the realisation that the Nazis could be beaten in the East massively increased Russia's popularity among the British people, a typical example being the September 1941 Tanks for Russia Week which aroused enthusiasm for 'Uncle Joe', as Joseph Stalin was now benevolently described. In February 1943 the Government promoted celebrations designed to mark the twenty-fifth anniversary of the Soviet Army.

# The BATTLE for CIVILISATION

The great majority of men and women are peaceable and law-abiding; only a few are criminals. And that is fortunate for civilisation, because if the bad out-numbered the good, the police would be faced with an impossible task, and neither life nor property would ever be safe. In the same way, most of the nations in the world are peaceable and orderly, desiring only to live as "good neighbours" with one another. The three "Axis Powers" are like three gangsters trying to hold up and rob all the rest of us. For years they have prepared their weapons and plotted together, so that they could strike without warning and gain the advantage of surprise. This was a very real and important advantage, and it gave them great successes at first—so great, indeed, that Hitler, after knocking out France in June, 1940, prophesied that he would be in London by the following August. However, the Battle of Britain put an end to that dream, and Hitler was forced, in his search for quick victories, to invade Russia instead—only to find that Moscow was equally difficult to reach. The civilised world is proving stronger than the gangsters after all.

The representation of the enemy in this 1942 leaflet bears a strong resemblance to some of the 'hate' propaganda produced in the First World War.

WORDS THAT DON'T RING TRUE!

"Italy's main function consists in drawing the best British Imperial forces like a magnet."

Signor Gayda to the Press, 8th March, 1941.

WORDS THAT DON'T RING TRUE!

"Danger from British air attacks, according to experience so far, does not make any action necessary."
D.N.B. (German Official News Agency),
16th October, 1940.

WORDS THAT DON'T RING TRUE!

"The relations between the Führer and the Duce are as cordial as those between two brothers."
"Asahi Shimbun" on Matsuoka's impression of his journey, quoted in a German broadcast to England,
23rd April, 1941.

Wit and subtlety in the 'Words That Don't Ring True' postcards, drawn by Nicholas Bentley. The cards shown were translated into French, Arabic and Persian.

More cluttered visual messages in which cartoons, statistics and quotes vie for attention.

Although the 'V for Victory' campaign was aimed at the occupied countries, it really took off in Britain. It is given a surprisingly modern treatment in this fold-out booklet.

**Nazi-German in 22 Lessons**

INCLUDING USEFUL INFORMATION FOR FÜHRERS, FIFTH COLUMNISTS, GAULEITERS AND QUISLINGS

LESSON 17
**ARYAN TYPE**
(Der arische Typus)

Blond like Hitler; slim like Göring; tall like Goebbels.

LESSON 7
**LIVING SPACE**
(Lebensraum)

A piece of fertile land or rich industrial territory occupied by someone else.

LESSON 20
**NO FURTHER TERRITORIAL AMBITION**
(Keine weiteren territorialen Forderungen)

A conversational phrase meaning "I intend to invade to-morrow."

Growing confidence in an Allied victory is reflected in these exuberantly satirical pamphlets.

# The GERMAN MILITARY LEXICON

G.P.D./288/76.

## Snow

A diabolical chemical invention of the Pluto-Bolshevist Democracies.

20

## Military Objective

An expression which denotes an object on which a bomb is dropped by the Luftwaffe. In Germany there are no military objectives.

12

## Blitzkrieg

A German technique for winning a world war in one— or at the most two—years.

2

'Have you ever seen a rat in a trap?' runs the commentary in the pamphlet *It's a Long Way to London*. 'Furious, despairing, it darts to every corner of its prison in turn . . . baffled, raging with the certainty of its doom.'

I would suggest that while the war is in its present stage it will not be difficult to canalise the public mind by distinguishing and confidently emphasising the difference between Russia and Bolshevism; by stating that what is suitable for the Slav temperament, which neither needs organisation, nor cares about it, and which is fantastic and poetic upon its outlook upon life, is not appropriate to the Anglo-Saxons who are, as a matter of fact, disinterested in political theories, except where they show a patent utility. If we allow the situation to develop for six months, it will be extremely difficult to canalise public opinion at all, but if we succeed in doing so, we shall only do so, at the expense of an open crusade. A crusade necessarily implies warfare, If we allow the situation to drift for more than six months it will, in my view, be entirely beyond control, and our problem then will not be to prevent a difficulty arising, but how to adjust the circumstances of life to what will be a novel situation based upon an accomplished fact.

R.H. Parker, director of MOI's Home Publicity Division, was very concerned to prevent the British public viewing Communism as a system that could serve their interests after the end of the war. (From a minute to the Director General of MOI, dated 15 July 1941)

In contrast the Ministry turned down Communist Party offers to provide speakers for official campaigns on increased production. In September 1941 it told the party leader, Harry Pollitt:

'I am to inform you that, having regard to the Communist Party's previous attitude towards the national war effort [when war broke out in 1939 the Party offered its support, then changed its policy later the same year, following pressure from Moscow, and finally reverted to its original position when Germany invaded the Soviet Union in 1941] the Minister does not feel that it is open to him to invite speakers drawn from the Communist Party to participate in this proposed campaign for increased production.'

# Undermining the enemy

As on the home publicity front, bureaucratic and political wrangling about overseas publicity marred the effectiveness of the operation in the initial months of the war. Eventually the Political Warfare Executive (PWE),

LONDON CALLING THE WORLD

by FRANK SINGLETON    1/- NET

*London Calling the World* promoted the BBC as the authoritative source of news throughout the occupied and the free world.

What are the other qualifications of the men who read aloud the news for twenty-four hours a day to the listening world? An Overseas News-reader is a different person from the man who reads the nine o'clock news in Britain. He is heard under widely varying conditions by people whose life, whose speech, whose habit, whose whole background are completely different from his own. His speech must be clear, friendly, and yet with the authority necessary to back a statement which comes from London. For London is the key word of all overseas bulletins. Several times in the course of the bulletin you will hear the announcer say, "This news bulletin comes to you from London"; or "This is London calling." And there must never be any doubt that London's news is truthful and authoritative.

From *London Calling the World.*

under the joint control of the Foreign Office, the military and the Ministry of Information, was placed in charge of policy on propaganda to enemy and enemy-occupied countries. Its aims were to undermine the enemy and to raise the morale of people suffering under Nazi occupation.

## BBC Overseas Radio Service

One of the PWE's chief vehicles was the BBC overseas radio service, which received guidance from the PWE on its output while retaining its editorial independence.

Since Britain was largely on the receiving end in the early part of the war, it was difficult to counter Nazi trumpeting of German military successes. The BBC, therefore, chose to challenge the Nazi concept of propaganda by providing accurate and reliable news and achieving credibility by frank admission of defeats, thereby gaining the trust of its audience; this proved crucial when the balance of war moved decisively in favour of Britain and its allies.

Once the Nazis were on the defensive, the BBC capitalised on the earlier bombast of Hitler and Goering by playing back extracts from their speeches and contrasting them with Germany's rapidly deteriorating military situation. To take one example, listeners were regularly reminded of Goering's guarantees that the Luftwaffe would not allow a single bomb to be dropped on the Ruhr and of Hitler's predictions of Germany's final victory. Similarly, when the Nazis complained about air raids on Germany, the BBC recalled the Führer's 1940 promise that he would eradicate Britain's cities.

Another technique was to exploit the German people's discontent with the corruption of the Nazi Party bosses by showing how they were feathering their own nests. The tone became more aggressive as the Allied victory became certain, one commentator accusing Goebbels of fighting by typewriter from his comfy armchair. Satire was also used to discredit the Nazi leaders. A weekly radio serial, *Corporal Adolf Hirnschal's Letters to His Wife*, contrasted Nazi propaganda with conditions suffered by the German soldier. In one letter, the corporal recorded that, when listening to a Hitler speech on the radio, the members of his company were lice-hunting in their clothing.

Broadcasts from London also focused on the occupied countries. The BBC programmes included regular time for broadcasters from these countries; the classic example was General de Gaulle and his main radio commentator, Maurice Schumann, who broadcast no fewer than 1,200 five-minute talks to the French people. One famous broadcaster in French was Winston Churchill, who, during one rehearsal, observed that his audience would not like the speech very much if it was in perfect French!

## V for Victory

The 'V for Victory' campaign was one of the BBC's most enduring contributions to the propaganda war, since, on the suggestion of a Belgian commentator, it combined the first letter of the French word for Victory and that of the Dutch word for Freedom. The campaign began in January 1941, with a broadcast for Belgium, and spread throughout Europe, resisters painting the V on public buildings. So successful was the campaign's impact that Goebbels himself took it up, unaware, it seems, of the irony of placing a massive V sign on the Eiffel Tower in Paris.

## Black Propaganda

The PWE was also responsible for covert black propaganda in the form of clandestine stations set up for Germany and each occupied country that appeared to be broadcasting from within that country. Perhaps the most notorious one was Gustav Siegfried Eins run by the journalist Sefton Delmer, who invented the chief character, a patriotic Prussian officer who railed against the Nazis by denouncing their corruption and depravity. The aim was to weaken the German war effort by exploiting and widening divisions among sections of the German population, particularly those between the Nazis and those officers hostile to Hitler. Another speciality was the spreading of rumour, including deception about Allied troop movements which was one of the keys to the success of the 1944 Normandy landings.

In addition to broadcasting, the PWE organised the printing of leaflets and miniature newspapers which were dropped over Europe by air, some by means of balloons. About 1,520 million leaflets were scattered on enemy or enemy-occupied territory. Black propaganda leaflets included posters that pretended to be of German origin; one supposedly advertised the work of the Nazi charity Winter Relief, by showing a cartoon of the SS leader, Heinrich Himmler – his victims in the background – rattling a collection box in one hand with a gun pointing from the other. One PWE sticker had four figures printed on it: 1918. Other material included false documents, like forged ration cards, designed to confuse the Nazi authorities.

# Britain under fire

The first use of aircraft to bomb civilians took place in the First World War, although on a very limited scale compared with 1939–45. Nevertheless, the impact was sufficient for military writers in the 1920s to paint an alarming scenario. The Government reacted by creating in 1924 a sub-committee of the Committee of Imperial Defence to look into the question of Air Raid Precautions (ARP). In 1935 it asked local government authorities to prepare for ARP and two years later ordered them to submit their plans for its approval.

## Civil Defence Volunteers

Shortly after Hitler's takeover of Austria in March 1938, the Home Secretary, Sir Samuel Hoare, broadcast to the nation, appealing for a million volunteers for emergency work. This campaign was given added impetus by the Nazi-created crisis over Czechoslovakia which led to the Munich agreement transferring the Sudeten Germans to German sovereignty. The distribution of about 38 million gas masks brought home to people the seriousness of Nazi threats to European peace. After the Munich agreement, a massive publicity drive took place to recruit ARP wardens and personnel for other services, such as the Auxiliary Fire Service. Posters appeared throughout the country and a booklet on protection of homes against air raids was delivered to every household. Further information was distributed on the use of gas masks and the need to black out windows.

In January 1939 the Government published its *National Service Handbook*, informing the population of the qualifications for service in the armed forces, nursing, the

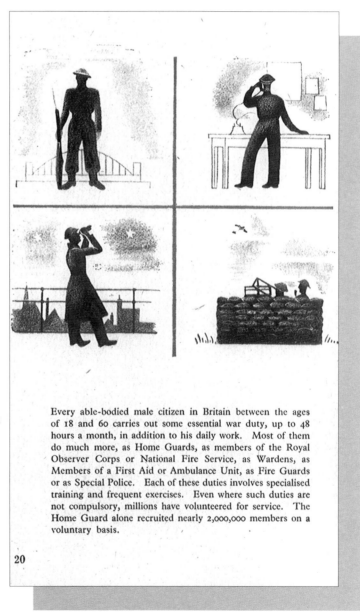

Every able-bodied male citizen in Britain between the ages of 18 and 60 carries out some essential war duty, up to 48 hours a month, in addition to his daily work. Most of them do much more, as Home Guards, as members of the Royal Observer Corps or National Fire Service, as Wardens, as Members of a First Aid or Ambulance Unit, as Fire Guards or as Special Police. Each of these duties involves specialised training and frequent exercises. Even where such duties are not compulsory, millions have volunteered for service. The Home Guard alone recruited nearly 2,000,000 members on a voluntary basis.

20

From *A People at War*.

Women's Land Army, the plane-watching Observer Corps and Civil Defence. Citizens could volunteer to become special police constables or auxiliary firemen. Others were needed for rescue and demolition squads, ambulance driving and communications. Above all, the Government wanted to have in place large numbers of trained air raid wardens able to deal with poison gas, contact the rescue services, administer first aid and help people find air raid shelters and rest centres.

Government appeals found a ready response, the Civil Defence services attracting over 1.5 million recruits by the beginning of the war.

In July 1939 a new Act strengthened the powers of local authorities on fire fighting, the building of shelters, and, where necessary, the evacuation of people from threatened areas. Many employers were required to organise ARP training and to provide shelters for their employees in large cities and other areas under threat.

## Coping with Air Raids

The first measure to help protect people from air attack was the blackout, which was enforced as soon as war broke out. Advance guidance was distributed to all homes in July 1939 in Public Information Leaflet No 2, recommending that 'the most convenient way of shutting in the light is to use close fitting blinds. These can be of any thick, dark coloured material such as dark blue or black or dark green glazed Holland, Lancaster or Italian cloth.' If these were not available, people were advised to obscure their windows by 'fixing up sheets of black paper or thick dark brown paper mounted on battens'.

Another concern of the authorities was gas attacks. The publicity machine leaped into action in September 1939, when the Ministry of Home Security issued its official instructions on how to deal with them: 'Always keep your gas mask with you – day and night. Learn to put it on quickly. Practise wearing it.' Once the wardens had sounded the warning gas rattles, people were told: 'Hold your breath. Put on mask wherever you are. Close window. If out of doors, take off hat, put on your mask. Turn up collar. Put on gloves or keep hands in pockets. Take cover in nearest building.' In October an official poster proclaimed: 'Hitler will give no warning – So always carry your gas mask.'

During the Phoney War period, before the astonishing German victories in the West in 1940, the carrying of gas masks steadily declined and in 1940 anxiety about gas attacks was

# what do I do...

## if a raid catches me in the street and I have to go to a public shelter?

I say to myself: This is where I keep quite calm and steady. It's human to be a bit nervous, but if I am, I'm not going to show it. I do not talk loudly, nor crack silly jokes, because that does *not* help others. And, much as I want to, I do not smoke — because it would make the shelter stuffy.

**Cut this out — and keep it!**

*Space presented to the Nation by The Brewers' Society;*
*Issued by The Ministry of Information.*

replaced by the very real experience of high explosive bombs falling in the period between September 1940 and July 1941 and killing 43,000 civilians. In July–August 1940, before the Blitz on cities began, the Ministry of Information placed advertisements encouraging rational behaviour in the face of frightening incidents. In the event of explosions:

> 'I keep a cool head. I take cover. I gather my family, with gas masks, and go quietly to my shelter or refuge room. I do not rush about alarming people. I remember that a lot of the noise is good noise - our guns firing at the enemy. And I remember the odds are thousands to one against my being hurt.'

In 1940 an official leaflet, 'Your Home as an Air Raid Shelter', advised: 'There are three ways in which you can provide your household with shelter. First you can buy a ready-made shelter to bury or erect in

From *A People at War*.

the garden. Secondly, you can have a shelter of brick or concrete built into or attached to your home. Thirdly you can improve the natural protection given by your house, by forming a refugee room . . . Almost no shelter is proof against a direct hit from a heavy bomb but the chances of your own house getting a direct hit are very small indeed.'

The most common home shelter was the Anderson shelter and was usually built in back gardens, providing considerable protection against flying glass and other debris caused by explosions. By September 1940 over 2 million were produced and in use. In addition, Morrison steel table shelters for use at home were manufactured. One 1940 Government leaflet noted the merits of a stout, strong table as a way of protecting people against raids by pointing out that people had often been rescued from a demolished house because such tables were able to bear the weight of a falling floor.

In 1941 the Ministry of Home Security issued advice to consumers prepared to invest in indoor air raid shelters marketed by private firms: 'The Ministry of Home Security is testing these, on application from the manufacturers. It is unwise to buy an indoor shelter for which the makers cannot produce a certificate of approval issued by the Ministry of Home Security.'

After the fire raid on London at the end of 1940, Home Secretary Herbert Morrison urged the Cabinet to introduce compulsory fire watching so that a watcher could be placed on the roof of every building. In the event the voluntary principle was retained, the Government being given additional powers to compel participation where necessary. The Fire Guard was formed in August 1941, its main counter to fires being the stirrup pump.

Practical advice rather than exhortation was much more important as a means of preserving the morale of people suffering serious hardships arising from incendiary bombs and fires. Although too late for

*Mrs. Mary Couchman is a 24-year-old warden in a small Kentish town. This picture was taken during an actual raid, when this brave woman crouched over three frightened children caught in the street, to protect them from bomb splinters with her own body.*

From *Eve in Overalls.*

(Above) Housewives learn how to take cover when tackling a dangerous incendiary bomb.
(Below, left) Two of Britain's women fire guards keep a look out.
(Right) learning the correct way to use a stirrup pump.

27

From *A People at War*.

many, one and a half million leaflets were distributed to fire fighters in 1941, giving information about the correct use of stirrup pumps and sandbags. Leaflets were also designed to assist people emerging from shelters. The 'After the Raid' leaflet advised people to go to rest centres if they had nowhere to sleep and eat; it concluded by saying that the Government, as well as fellow citizens and neighbours, were anxious to see that front line fighters were looked after.

Not that official advice was always taken. Publicity campaigns to promote the merits of surface brick air raid shelters in London were often disregarded since people felt safer in underground tube stations. Moreover, the first days of the Blitz had a very serious effect on morale, coupled as they were with inadequate deep shelters, lack of facilities for sleep and insanitary conditions. Churchill acted swiftly by appointing Morrison as Home Secretary to provide further impetus to solving problems arising from the Blitz and so restore public morale. Permanent canteen facilities were now provided for those in shelters and by the spring of 1941 most people in London shelters were sleeping in reasonable conditions.

A still from *Total War in Britain*, a 1945 MOI film produced by Paul Rotha, with a commentary by John Mills.

Five-minute films were commissioned by the Ministry of Information to boost morale by highlighting the efforts of individuals, for example telephonists carrying on working near unexploded bombs and war workers in factories turning out more and more weapons. One of the most famous wartime documentaries was Humphrey Jennings's film *London Can Take It*, showing the dome of St Paul's Cathedral undamaged in the skyline. Jennings's memorial to the courage of London's firefighters, *Fires Were Started*, was produced by the Crown Film Unit for the Ministry of Information. This showed the experience and courage of a fire crew during a single night in the Luftwaffe's blitz on London. Made in 1942 and featuring real firemen, it was shot on location with a fire staged in St Katherine's Dock. It received enthusiastic reviews by film critics in the press.

In the same year the Ministry of Information produced an official illustrated booklet, *Front Line 1940–41: The Official Story of the Civil Defence*, which provided a detailed account of the brave efforts made by people to combat the effects of air raids. Morale-boosting pictures showed a milk delivery man negotiating a passage across the ruins and a postman emptying a pillar box surrounded by debris. Praise was showered on Fleet Street where, during every night of the Blitz, the main editions of the newspapers were printed. This was, the booklet wrote, 'the reply of a free press to Hitler; an apt piece of symbolism'.

All those appearing in the 1943 film *Fires Were Started*, directed and scripted by Humphrey Jennings, were members of the Fire Service carrying out their normal duties.

*Front Line* ended with an uplifting conclusion:

'It was the conscious privilege of the British people to teach [the enemy] two lessons – the earliest of all those which the free peoples of the world will yet enforce upon him. The first was the Battle of Britain, when the finest squadrons of his chief weapon of terror were brought low by lesser numbers of freer men. The second was the defeat of his air bombardment by a general and widespread power of thought, action and endurance, based upon the clear consciousness of a just cause.'

It also quoted comments made by Churchill in April 1941:

'I see the damage done by the enemy attacks; but I also see, side by side with the devastation and amid the ruins, quiet, confident, bright and smiling eyes, beaming with a consciousness of being associated with a cause far higher and wider than any human or personal issue. I see the spirit of an unconquerable people.'

## Beating the Invader

Following the successful German blitzkrieg and the defeat of France in 1940, there were understandable fears about the possibility of a German invasion, especially when Goering's airforce attempted to destroy British air defences before switching to air raids against London and other big cities. So strong were these fears that a leaflet, 'Beating the Invader', was issued by the Ministry of Information and distributed throughout the country. It was prefaced by a message from Churchill emphasising that there would be most violent fighting where the enemy landed, or attempted to land:

'Not only will there be the battles when the enemy tries to come ashore, but afterwards there will fall upon his lodgments very heavy British counter-attacks, and all the time the lodgments will be under the heaviest attack by British bombers . . . The Home Guard [see p. 47], supported by strong mobile columns wherever the enemy's numbers require it, will immediately come to grips with the invaders, and there is little doubt will soon destroy them.'

The leaflet told people to 'STAND FIRM' if fighting broke out in their neighbourhood:

'Keep indoors or in your shelter until the battle is over. If you can have a trench ready in your garden or field, so much the better . . . But if you are at work, or if you have special orders, carry on as long as possible and only take cover when danger approaches'.

If faced with an enemy tank or a few enemy soldiers, this did not mean that the enemy was in control: 'What you have seen may be a party sent on in advance, or stragglers from the main body who can easily be rounded up.'

In areas some way from the fighting, people were urged to 'CARRY ON' by staying in their district and working in their shops, offices, factories or farms. The leaflet explained that advice and orders would be given by the police and ARP wardens:

'You will generally know your policeman and your ARP wardens by sight, and can trust them. With a bit of common sense you can tell if a soldier is really British or only pretending to be so. If in doubt ask a policeman, or ask a soldier whom you know personally.'

The population was reassured about food: 'If you have already laid in a stock of food, keep it for a real emergency; but do not add to it. The Government has made arrangements for food supplies.' As for news, normal services would continue and in case of need emergency measures would bring news to the people. 'But if there should be some temporary breakdown in news supply, it is very important that you should not listen to rumours or pass them on, but should wait till real news comes through again.'

## Anti-gossip Campaigns

During the first year of the war, a major theme of publicity was the need to prevent information reaching the enemy, a fear influenced by the widespread talk in books and the media about the alleged operations of Nazi Fifth Columns in countries invaded by Germany. The campaign opened with a Ministry of Information warning: 'DO NOT DISCUSS ANYTHING WHICH MIGHT BE OF NATIONAL IMPORTANCE. THE CONSEQUENCE OF ANY SUCH INDISCRETION MAY BE THE LOSS OF MANY LIVES.'

Newspaper advertisement.

A lighter touch was applied in the memorable posters commissioned by the Ministry and drawn by the artist Kenneth Bird under the name 'Fougasse' on the theme 'Careless Talk Costs Lives'. One showed two women – Hitler and a bemedalled Goering sitting behind them – with one saying to the other, 'You never know who's listening.' Fougasse also drew a man and woman seated at the dinner table, one saying to the other 'Of course there's no harm in your knowing!', an eager Hitler crouching under the table with his notebook. Some 2.5 million copies of these posters were printed and brought a bit of humour into the Government's until then rather earnest publicity.

Other wartime slogans on this theme were 'Keep it under your hat' and 'Be like Dad, keep Mum', the latter arousing criticism among feminists, including Dame Edith Summerskill.

Edwin Embleton, a Ministry official, recalls that Fougasse gave his services free as a contribution to the war effort. The Ministry's demand for cartoons of Hitler also gave scope for other artists Embleton commissioned, among others, the young Wally Fawkes – the present political cartoonist of the *Observer* – to draw caricatures of the Führer for use in official publications.

Less inspiring was the short-lived 'Silent Column' campaign which Churchill requested in early July 1940 in order to deal with rumours. The Ministry of Information's newspaper advertisements urged the population to 'Join Britain's Silent Column':

> 'You will wear no uniform, you will not spend nights on lonely duty. Your only weapons will be your commonsense, your ears and your tongue . . . The country asks you to join the Silent Column - the great body of sensible people who know when not to talk and who will, in the event of an invasion, stop the rumours that lead to confusion . . . It will not be easy – to be a loyal member of the Silent Column you'll need a great deal of self-control and courage to speak up in order to keep dangerous speech down.'

The advertisement added:

> 'Most people talk dangerously without realising that they are doing so. Tactfully point out that what they are saying should be left unsaid. If somebody starts talking rumour take out an old envelope and start writing down what they are saying.'

Another implored:

> 'IF YOU KNOW
> . . . exactly where a bomb fell
> . . . what time it fell
> . . . what the bomb just missed
> . . . how many aeroplanes there were
> . . . what they were trying to hit
> . . . which direction they came from
> . . . which district they were over
> . . . KEEP IT TO YOURSELF and make others do the same . . .'

*Facing page:* A 1942 poster by Abram Games, a young but influential graphic artist who had enlisted as a pri but was soon summoned to become the Official War Office Poster Desi

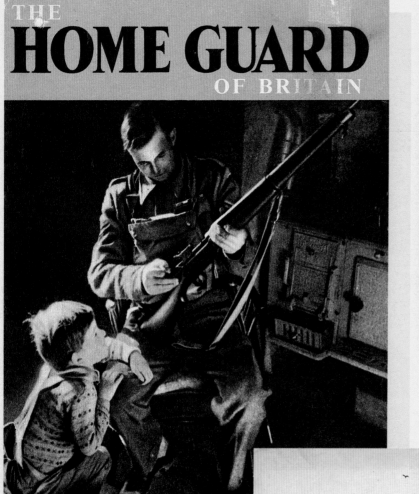

A postcard issued to Allied merchant navy crews.

The *Home Guard of Britain* paid tribute to over a million and a half men 'who are just as much soldiers of the Regular Army as the Grenadier Guards.' (Churchill)

Hitler eavesdropping was a popular image in many anti-careless talk posters.

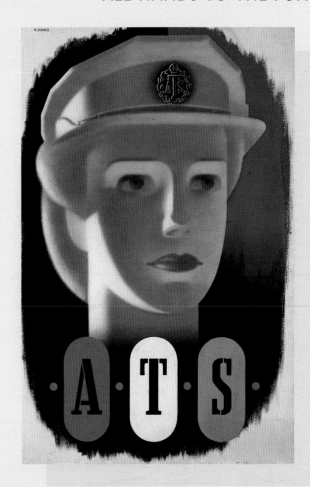

Abram Games's first recruitment poster for the women's Auxiliary Territorial Service (left) caused a furore after a complaint by the MP Thelma Cazalet. Ernest Bevin, Minister of Labour, ordered the 'Blonde Bombshell' to be withdrawn. Games's 1944 poster (right) offered a staider image.

There was no such pressure on the unknown artist to change the face in this poster. Was the woman on the left felt to be too masculine, or simply lacking in urgency?

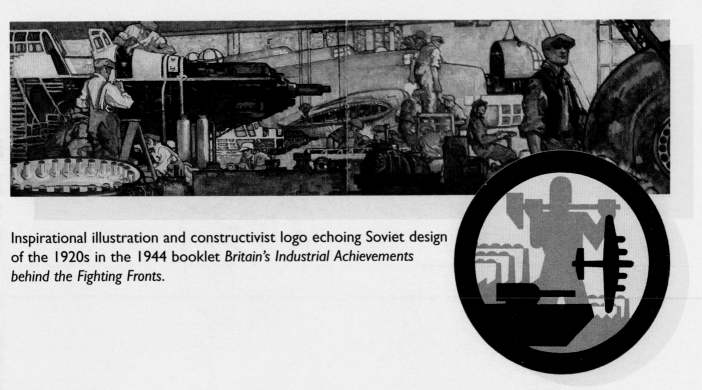

Inspirational illustration and constructivist logo echoing Soviet design of the 1920s in the 1944 booklet *Britain's Industrial Achievements behind the Fighting Fronts.*

*It might hold up the others if I was late at my work*

there are NO SLACKERS in Britain to-day!

The statistics behind Britain's industrial effort make impressive reading: £50,000 of munitions produced every minute; 275,000 fighting vehicles manufactured every year . . . and the list went on.

BRITISH GUNS—NO. I

THE WOMEN BEHIND THE GUNS

In Britain's newest ordnance factory 80 per cent of the workers are women. Two or three years ago many of them had never been inside a factory.

For Victory

GPD 365 /21 /6

By 1944, 7 million women were employed in essential industries or in the Services.

Cartoonist H.M. Bateman brought social pressure to bear on those who squandered fuel, while Clive Uptton opted for a simpler visual equation.

Warnings to resist the siren song of the swastika-strewn Squander Bug appeared in newspapers and magazines, and on posters.

Families were urged to save scraps for feeding pigs, poultry and rabbits, bearing in mind that 'peeling potatoes is a peacetime luxury.' (*The Little Less*)

*The Little Less*, illustrated by the popular *Punch* cartoonist Fougasse, combined 'witty drawings and truly staggering statistics' to encourage readers to make economies.

The Silent Column did not work, as Harold Nicolson pointed out in his diary in July 1940: 'There is no doubt our anti-rumour campaign has been a ghastly failure. . . . Partly because our silence campaign and the prosecutions for gossip which have taken place in the country have caused justifiable irritation. And partly because the country is in a bad state of nerves during this lull before the storm.' Churchill drew the appropriate conclusion by publicly axing the campaign at the end of July.

The Ministry of Information was also concerned about the impact of German propaganda broadcasts by William Joyce, known as Lord Haw-Haw, who did his best to spread rumour and despondency. In July 1940 the Ministry issued an advertisement in its 'What Do I Do?' series in press space presented to the nation by the Brewers' Society:

> 'What do I do . . . if I come across German or Italian broadcasts when tuning my wireless? I say to myself: "Now this blighter wants me to listen to him. Am I going to do what he wants?" I remember that German lies over the air are like parachute troops dropping on Britain – they are all part of the plan to get us down – which they won't. I remember nobody can trust a word the Haw-Haws say. So, just to make them waste their time, I switch 'em off or tune 'em out." '

## Evacuees

One of the first measures taken by the Government after war broke out was the implementation of plans to evacuate young children from

Evacuees on board a London Transport bus from *Transport Goes to War*, a 1942 booklet published by MOI for the Ministry of Transport.

*Left :* **Sticks instead of rifles !** The men are awkward and stiff. Suppleness will come with training and the rifle is soon to be a familiar friend.

**They begin** to take the shape and form of soldiers.

From *The Home Guard of Britain.*

large urban areas under threat from air attack and to billet them in other peoples' houses. These plans were backed up by publicity in the form of posters.

One poster, showing a picture of a brother and sister, read 'MOTHERS. Send them out of London. Give them a chance of greater safety and health'. And another, illustrated by a cartoon of Hitler urging evacuees to return, warned: 'Don't do it Mother. Leave the children where they are.' Publicity also paid tribute to foster parents willing to take evacuated children.

In 1940 a Scottish Office advertisement expressed thanks to the 20,000 families who were greatly helping the country by looking after such children. It also appealed for new volunteers: 'But many new volunteers are needed – to share in the present task and to be ready for any crisis that may come. Won't you be one of them? . . . You will be doing a real service for the nation. You may be saving a child's life.'

# Home Guard

Perhaps the most successful publicity campaign in 1940 was that leading to the formation of the Local Defence Volunteers (LDV), later renamed the Home Guard, and satirised more recently as 'Dad's Army.' Four days after the beginning of the German offensive in Western Europe, War Secretary Anthony Eden broadcast on the BBC Home Service appealing for male volunteers between 17 and 65 to come forward to serve as part-time soldiers. Within 24 hours some 250,000 men responded and by the end of June volunteers numbered nearly 1.5 million. The Ministry of Information had a platoon of 180 and Lord Woolton, the Food Minister, found 62 members of his Bacon and Ham Division on parade during his first inspection.

A week after Eden's broadcast the Government announced that the first task of the LDV was observation and the provision of information about German parachutists. The others were to prevent movement by German soldiers landed from the air and to assist in patrolling and protecting vulnerable spots. Observation posts were soon set up on hilltops and places like church towers. The author J.B. Priestley described his experiences – in somewhat romantic vein – during one of his BBC *Postscript* talks, broadcast on 16 June 1940:

> 'The post is on top of a high down, with a fine view over a dozen wide parishes. The men I met up there the other night represented a good cross section of English rural life; we had a parson, a bailiff, a builder, farmers and farm labourers . . . The sentries took their posts . . . Nothing much happened for a time. A green light that seemed to defy all black-out regulations turned out to be merely an extra large and luminous glow-worm; the glow-worms, poor ignorant little creatures, don't know there's a war on and so continue lighting themselves up. A few searchlights went stabbing through the dusk and then faded . . .'

An official publication, *The Home Guard of Britain*, described the Home Guard as 'probably the most democratic army in the world . . . An army in whose ranks mingle labourers and architects, editors and bricklayers, engineers and shepherds.' The Guard, said the booklet, consisted of 'two million men who are determined to stand their ground and fight – yes, and would like Hitler to give them the opportunity to fight – until the roads are blocked with German corpses or the way is barred with their own.'

They clatter through the Sunday morning silence of the factory towns . . . .

From *The Home Guard of Britain*.

# Mobilising the people

The experience of the First World War had shown the need to mobilise Britain's industrial and labour resources. During the Phoney War period unemployment was still a problem and there were still 700,000 out of work when Ernest Bevin took office as Minister of Labour and National Service. Adequate rearmament for later offensives against the enemy could only occur if the country's economy was organised for it.

The new Government reacted immediately, new regulations giving the Minister of Labour power 'to direct any person in the United Kingdom to perform any such services as he might specify'. Nevertheless, Bevin preferred to act by persuasion in order to carry the people with him and to use the powers as a last resort. He immediately gained the co-operation of the employers and unions,

Workers get on their bikes, in the booklet *War Job*.

*Above :* These pre-fabricated huts were erected in 10 days by men of a Flying Squad of builders. Efficient organisation of these mobile building units makes it possible to provide immediate accommodation for war workers under any circumstances.

*Right :* Another type of Flying Squad. These are skilled industrial workers who have volunteered to work in any part of the country where their services are specially required to reinforce local labour forces.

a joint body being set up by them to advise him on issues that would inevitably arise from the legislation. He also obtained agreement from the unions that they would abandon traditional demarcations between workers and voluntarily allow large numbers of semi-skilled and unskilled workers into the armaments factories

The importance of labour mobilisation was recognised by Churchill, who made Bevin a member of the War Cabinet in October 1940. Publicity directed at the workers traded on Bevin's achievements as a trade union leader: 'For twenty years "Ernie" Bevin has occupied a unique place in the hearts of the British working man and woman – ever since that day in 1920 when, famous as the "dockers' KC", he made an historic 11-hour speech defending the rights of working people . . . Throughout this heroic struggle, the British working man and woman . . . put their liberties into the hands of Mr Bevin to use them as he would, with a willingness beyond the wildest dreams of the Continental tyrant.'

Early in 1941 legislation was passed requiring all men over 41 and women over 20 to register for employment in war work. In March 1941 the Minister of Labour was given authority to schedule a factory as engaged on essential national work, which meant that workers could not leave or be dismissed without the consent of the Ministry. Employers for their part had to pay a guaranteed weekly wage and make provision for training and welfare.

## Conscripting Women for War Work

One of the most controversial measures taken by Bevin was the decision to conscript women for war work because of the shortage of labour, although public opinion began to move in favour of compulsion given the scale of the effort required to defeat Nazi Germany and the need for all people to be treated fairly. In December 1941 legislation was passed providing for the conscription of women into the womens' armed forces and in areas like civil defence and industry. They could, however, choose which service to enter. The new law applied to those between 20 and 30, but excluded married women.

In 1942 publicity urged women to become 'part of the DRIVING FORCE behind the Offensive' by joining the ATS (Auxiliary Territorial Service) and the WAAF (Women's Auxiliary Air Force). One advertisement showed a picture of a woman driving a convoy of supplies for the battle fronts:

> 'She is one of the women whom the whole world acclaims now as part of Britain's great fighting strength. Thousands more like her are needed to release men for the Offensive.'

Another portrayed a group of women in charge of an anti-aircraft battery:

> 'Women of the ATS handle this job magnificently. Working side-by-side with men, facing hardship and danger as comrades in arms, they defend the villages and cities they love, and the people who live and work in them. Thousands more women are needed for this work – needed urgently.'

Although most official posters were commissioned by the Ministry of Information, the War Office had its own poster designer, Abram Games, responsible for about 100 posters for members of the armed forces, dealing with issues like fitness, security, weapons and welfare. One of his first efforts was a recruiting poster for the ATS which lead to attacks in Parliament, much coverage in the press and its subsequent withdrawal on the grounds that it was too glamorous, although the general public had a much more favourable reaction. As Mr Games explains: 'The press got hold of it because it was an opportunity to contrast the glamour of the poster with the image of the MP, Mrs Cazalet, who complained about it.'

**EVE in overalls**

by Arthur Wauters, Official Delegate of the Belgian Government to the British Ministry of Information

From *Women in Shipbuilding*,
published by the Ministry of Labour
and National Service
in 1943.

## Foreword

IN this fourth year of war the shipbuilding industry is faced with an expanding programme of construction at a time when there is little prospect of appreciable increase in the male labour force. The stage has now been reached when the industry can get the necessary additional labour only if it is prepared to employ women to a far greater extent than hitherto. In recent months women have entered the shipyards in increasing numbers and have proved their worth. In most yards they are already employed as cleaners, general labourers and as assistants to craftsmen.

IT is not sufficiently well known, however, that given suitable training and encouragement they are able to undertake many of the duties of the craftsmen themselves. This booklet illustrates the types of skilled and semi-skilled work on which women have been successfully tried out in some shipyards and draws attention to the possibilities of employing them on a wider range of occupations than hitherto thought suitable.

WORKING ON A WARSHIP, they
are welding the superstructure.

'More and more in the future of Great Britain, women will play the role which they deserve, and they will play it well. Britain, defending her freedom, has contracted an immense debt of gratitude to the women.' *Eve in Overalls*

*A Women's Royal Naval Service dispatch rider carries an urgent message to an Officer of a destroyer, which has just returned to port after patrol duties.*

E. O. 2 S. A

**A postwoman makes her daily rounds.**

**Two " Radio Wrens," who fly naval aircraft to test the radio equipment.**

'Our women tipped the scales of war.' Ernest Bevin, Minister of Labour and National Service, in *50 Facts About the Women of Britain at war.*

By the end of 1942 more than 8.5 million women were registered for national service. And in mid-1943 women constituted 40 per cent of all employees in the aircraft industry, 35 per cent in the engineering industry and 52 per cent in factories making explosives and chemicals.

The British mobilisation for total war turned out to be far more successful than that of Germany and was largely built on the principle of consent, unlike the Nazi war effort, which relied on the ruthless exploitation of millions of forced labourers from the occupied countries.

# Fighting fit

Adequate food supplies were recognised to be a key factor in the maintenance of morale. The Ministry of Food was one of the largest spenders on publicity, issuing a constant flow of leaflets, press advertisements and short films explaining the rationing system and providing information on wartime recipes and ways of making limited supplies go round.

## Digging for Victory

The Ministry of Agriculture was responsible for waves of publicity designed to increase land under cultivation on farms and on allotments. One of the most famous slogans of the war was 'Dig for Victory', the campaign getting off to an immediate start in early October 1939 with a broadcast from the Minister of Agriculture pointing out that half a million new allotments would provide enough vegetables to feed a million adults and one and a half million children for eight months out

From *A People at War*.

The pursuits and interests of the British people are many and varied, but one interest is shared by all—the love of a beautiful garden. In a British home the living room looks out on a neat lawn, trim flower beds and roses in bloom. But to release land for essential crops the people know that they must grow their own vegetables. So spades have been thrust into the carefully tended lawns, the rose bushes have been ruthlessly torn out, flower beds have been turned into vegetable plots. Allotments are being cultivated on every spare piece of ground available.

of twelve: 'So. Let's get going. Let "Dig for Victory" be the motto of everyone with a garden and of every able-bodied man and woman capable of digging an allotment in their spare time.' One early piece of publicity urged: 'Beg, buy or borrow a spade and Dig for Victory . . . . Step on it – make every garden a VICTORY GARDEN.'

As part of the campaign the Ministry of Agriculture published many leaflets about the cultivation of vegetables such as potatoes, onions, leeks, shallots, peas, beans and cabbages. Important advice was also given on pest and disease control.

The campaign caught the imagination, as well as the appetites, of the population, the number of allotments in England and Wales shooting up from 815,000 in 1939 to a peak of 1,450,000 by 1944. In addition, many front gardens soon sprouted rows of cabbages, runner beans and other vegetables.

The massive contribution made by farmers, too, was of vital importance to feeding the nation, as one slogan made clear: 'Ploughing on FARMS is as vital as ARMS.' By 1944 arable land had increased by 50 per cent and pasture land by 66 per cent. Moreover, output of wheat nearly doubled and that of potatoes soared by over 100 per cent. Farmers were helped by the formation of the Women's Land Army, founded in 1939 to attract volunteers for agricultural work. The Army was organised entirely by women and by 1943 there were 90,000 members.

From *Eve in Overalls*.

# Food Rationing

As the war continued, Britain's external trade was gravely disrupted, a particular menace being the attacks on merchant shipping by German submarines in the Atlantic; this continued to be a major threat well into 1943. The result was that many commodities were unobtainable or in short supply. The Government, therefore, decided that the fairest way of dealing with the problem was rationing, a step widely welcomed by the people and crucial to the maintenance and the pursuit of the war effort.

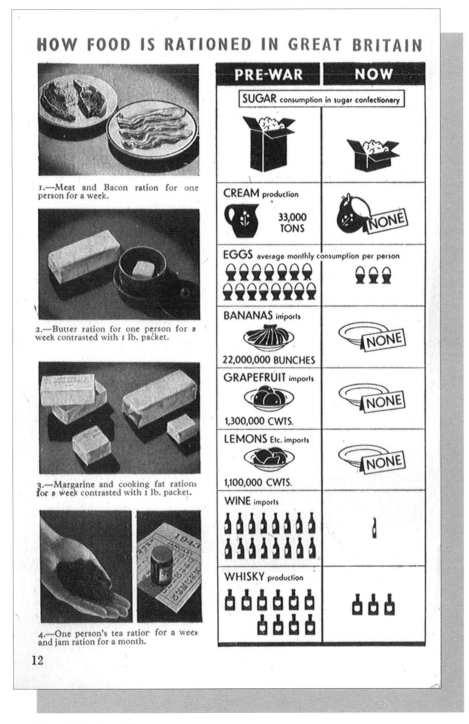

From *A People at War*.

Food rationing started early in January 1940 for bacon, ham, sugar and butter. Later in the year rationing covered meat, tea, margarine and cooking fat. In 1941 it was the turn of cheese, jam and marmalade. Some foods which were not on ration coupons, such as tinned meat and fruit, quickly became unavailable. The Ministry of Food reacted to these shortages at the end of 1941 by introducing a widely welcomed points rationing scheme, under which the ration book holder received a number of points, the Ministry giving points values to the foods covered by the scheme.

Home Intelligence reports indicate that the rationing system was approved by the public. In July–August 1941 they reported that

> 'there appears to be little uneasiness concerning the general food situation and the large majority still feels that on the whole it is "getting a fair deal". . . it is rather on the "day-to-day difficulties of getting domestic supplies" that dissatisfaction continues'.

In September 1941 it reported that 'Lord Woolton's recent speeches are welcomed as having done much to show people how fortunate we are compared with other countries.'

## The Kitchen Front

The popular Minister of Food, Lord Woolton, summed up the food situation in a Royal Horticultural Society booklet published in 1942:

> 'This is a Food War. Every extra row of vegetables in allotments saves shipping. If we grow more Potatoes, we need not import so much wheat...We must grow our own Onions. We can no longer import ninety per cent of them, as we did before the war. The vegetable garden is also our National Medicine Chest – it yields a large proportion of the vitamins which protect us against infection . . . The battle on the Kitchen Front cannot be won without help from the Kitchen Garden.'

The Ministry of Food emphasised the need to eat more of the foods that could be produced at home. A Ministry leaflet asserted that no country in the world grew vegetables better than Britain and 'probably no country in the world cooks them worse.' It therefore urged cooks to stop boiling the nutrition out of their vegetables and warned makers of highly seasoned sauces that, once the British palate was accustomed to good eating, people would be 'content with the delicate flavour of well-cooked vegetables' which were 'one of our most important sources of health and strength'.

The humble carrot became a focus of this publicity effort, a Ministry leaflet commenting: 'The carrot is one of our most valuable root vegetables, for it contains protective substances which increase our resistance to infection and help us to see in the blackout.' The potato became the subject of exhortations by the Ministry:

> 'There is no vegetable more useful than the homely potato. Potatoes are a cheap source of energy, and they are one of the foods that help to protect us from illness . . . Eat them in place of bread and other cereals wherever possible, and you help to save shipping space . . . Always cook them in their skins.'

As for salads, they had 'wonderful powers' to 'give us vim and vigour'. When arranging salads, the Ministry urged, 'remember that a bright gleam here and there in the greenery is tempting, and where the eye leads, good digestion follows.' The harvests of the hedgerow were widely publicised, the Ministry extolling the merits of blackberry leaf tea: 'This tea may be infused like ordinary tea . . . or it may be used half and half with ordinary tea to eke out the ration.'

The phrase 'the Kitchen Front' proved to be one of the most successful of wartime publicity concepts. Press advertisements pointed out that 'Food is a munition of war. Don't waste it'. The BBC broadcast daily Ministry of Food talks on the Kitchen Front. In addition, the BBC radio comedy characters Gert and Daisy, played by Elsie and Doris Waters, published a popular wartime recipe book which, among other things, warned against bread wastage: 'So, if you ever forget, do what Daisy did. She chucked a bit of bread out of the window, suddenly remembered, and rushed downstairs and caught it before it reached the ground.'

The cartoon characters Dr Carrot and Potato Pete regularly appeared in the press and women's magazines. The recipes for carrot flan and carrot marmalade were promoted by the Ministry but not to universal public acclaim.

## 'Food Facts'

From the summer of 1940 to the end of the war, the Ministry of Food published weekly 'Food Facts' press advertisements, including information about recipes. The first set the tone:

> 'Grow fit not fat on your war diet! Make full use of the fruit and vegetables in season. Cut out "extras"; cut out waste; don't eat more than you need. You'll save yourself money, you'll save valuable cargo space which is needed for munitions, and you'll feel fitter than you ever felt before.'

**60** To save shipping, imports of animal food-stuffs have been reduced from 8,750,000 tons to 1,250,000 tons. Larger quantities of fodder crops grown at home have helped to maintain milk production, but meat, poultry and eggs have had to be curtailed.

From *100 Facts About the United Kingdom's War Effort.*

The advertisement spelled out the correct way to make tea, which was then rationed:

'You can save that "extra one for the pot" if you get the best out of your tea. So, remember that (1) as soon as the water is boiling really fast you should be ready with the well-warmed tea-pot; (2) the tea-pot should come to the kettle, not the kettle to the tea-pot; (3) you should give the tea enough time to brew, and stir it just before pouring. If you do all this your ration will go further.'

One Food Facts ad published in 1942 celebrated the fitness of the country:' When athletes go into training they eat to a plan. With the country all out to win the war, of course it must eat to a plan. Today's Menu for Victory? More potatoes, less bread; and your full ration of cheese.' Under the headline BREAD INTO BATTLE, Food Facts No 99 praised the housewife's contribution to the war effort but warned:

' . . . she's falling down on one thing  perhaps she thinks it trifling – the daily waste of bread. Too many crusts are being thrown away . . . Wheat takes the lion's share of our shipping space. Even if the daily waste of bread is as little as half an ounce per head of the population: that means a waste of fifteen loaves a second, and thirty shiploads of flour in a year – a whole convoy! Bread into Battle? Yes indeed – and that's why every half-ounce saved is half the battle.'

One proposal the Ministry of Food did not take up.

Economy and wit in a 1942 poster by Abram Games.

Mrs Sew and Sew was the supreme exponent of 'Make Do and Mend'. The booklet of the same name appeared in 1943. It was intended, said President of the Board of Trade Hugh Dalton, 'to help you get the last possible ounce of wear out of all your clothes and household things.'

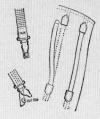

24     MAKE DO AND MEND

## CORSETS

**To Take In a Belt.** A belt that has become too big for you owing to the rubber perishing can be re-shaped by making a strong seam down either side and down the centre of the back, or at the damaged point. You must make the ridge of the seam on the outer side of the belt, otherwise it will be most uncomfortable to wear. You should use a sewing machine for this if you possibly can. Turn the garment inside out, tack the new seam, run the machine down it, and cut away the surplus material before turning it to the right side and making a second row of stitching to take in the raw edges.

**To Let Out a Belt.** Insert a piece of strong material down each side, machining it on-to the corset.

**When Corset Bones Break.** Never throw away corset bones, suspenders or parts of these, and save all ribbons, tapes, hooks and buttons. Then, if you break the bones in your corsets, you can make little pockets as shown in the accompanying diagram, and

slip in those taken from another pair. It is well worth making corset bones removable as this saves them from wear in washing.

**To Replace Corset Accessories.** If the elastic on the suspenders of a new pair of corsets is too short, lengthen it before you wear the belt by adding a short piece of tape, otherwise you may tear your stockings. If you lose the back portion of a suspender remember that a small, fabric-covered button on a length of tape can be used to take its place.

## DRESSES

**Colour Contrast Renovations.** When sleeves, front panels or underarms are worn out, contrasting sleeves or panels can look very attractive. Use up oddments of material from another worn garment if possible.

**To Widen a Bodice.** Widen a frock which has become too narrow in the bust, by opening the bodice and letting in a plastron of another material. You can make it oval or rectangular in shape, or you could attach a band of the new material to either side of the bodice and fasten it down the centre front with a line of buttons to give a waistcoat effect.

**To Lengthen a Dress.** A dress which has become too short in washing or cleaning can be lengthened by letting a band of material, in self-colour, or in a contrasting shade, into the skirt between waist and hip-line. Dirndl skirts, in particular, lend themselves to this treatment. If you use a contrasting colour bind the neckline with the same material, or add patch pockets to the bodice.

TURN OUT AND RENOVATE     25

**Two Old Dresses into a Coat-Frock.** Here is an idea for a dark woollen dress that is worn in front and is too tight for you. Open it from neck to hem and finish the edges neatly, turning them in and rounding them up to the neck, unless you like to turn down the points at the neck as revers. Then use the best part of the silk from an old printed dress or any other material you may have in a contrasting colour, and gather it in a panel down the front, fastening it under the edges of the dark material to give the effect of a Redingote worn over a dress. This is very suitable for maternity wear.

You could use the bodice of the figured silk frock to make a blouse. It will probably be worn under the arms, or you wouldn't be cutting it up, but there should be ample material left over in the skirt after making the panel for the coat-frock to put in new short sleeves and a yoke to the blouse.

**Worn Elbows.** Cut worn sleeves away above the elbow and finish them off with neat cuffs, taken from the lower part of the sleeve, that follow the line of the collar or neck trimming. If you want to keep long sleeves, cut away the worn parts at the elbow and insert oblong pieces of matching material, or even contrasting colours in decorative shapes.

**Skirt from a Dress.** A useful skirt can be made from a dress, the bodice of which is past repair. Cut it away at the waist, make a side placket and mount it on a petersham band. The best parts from the bodice can be cut into a belt to finish the waistline or to make patch pockets on the hips. Pocket patches would hide any defects in the front.

## GLOVES

Wear gloves only to keep warm, and when you take them off put them in your pocket or bag. Thousands of gloves are lost every year.

**Worn Fingers.** The underside of glove fingers and the palms often wear out when the backs are still in good condition. Using a glove pattern, make new undersides of thin toning or contrasting felt or woollen fabric, and stitch them on to the leather backs.

## MEN'S CLOTHING INTO WOMEN'S

Here are some ways in which a man's unwanted garments can be converted to your own use, if you are

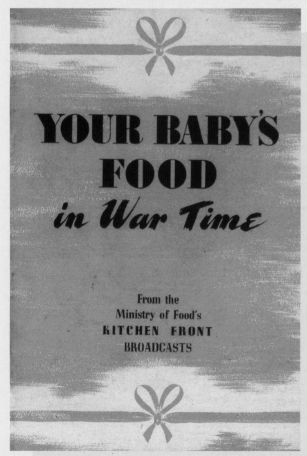

'I know some people say tea sends them all of a dither, but those people are usually all of a dither anyway.' Dr Charles Hill's radio broadcasts served up dietary advice – made palatable by his exuberant common sense – to listeners grappling with rationing and shortages.

A *People at War* highlighted the fortitude of the people by means of statistics showing the extent of their sacrifice.

| PRE-WAR | NOW | PRE-WAR | NOW |
|---|---|---|---|
| **VALUE OF MEAT USED** (per average week) | | **EGGS USED** (per average week) | |
| £281 worth | £16·7·0 worth | 9,100 Eggs | Less than 70 Eggs |
| **SUGAR USED** (per average week) | | | |
| 700 lbs. of sugar | 180 lbs. of sugar | | |
| **BUTTER USED** (per average week) | | **CREAM USED** (per average week) | |
| 392 lbs. of butter | 77 lbs. of butter | 40 gallons of Cream | NONE — Only SYNTHETIC Cream. (10 galls.) |

Diagrams show the pre-war and present day consumption of staple foods in three of London's most famous luxury restaurants—meat in Simpson's, sugar and eggs in Claridge's, butter and cream in the Ritz.

Potato Pete was the star of numerous recipes and radio jingles, and fostered something of a mania for planting potatoes.

One of several H.M. Bateman posters aimed at combating droplet infection. The Chief Medical Officer calculated that the loss of working hours from colds and flu was the equivalent of 3,500 tanks, 1,000 bombers and 1,000,000 rifles a year.

*How to Keep Well in Wartime* contained a wealth of good advice, much of it as current now as it was then: cut down smoking, drink more water and don't rush potty training.

RUBBER
helps to make
TYRES

Fougasse exploits the visual device of 'morphing' to show how hot water bottles can be transformed
into tyres.

# Help put the lid on Hitler
## BY SAVING YOUR
## OLD METAL AND PAPER

Everyone could contribute something to the war effort: if each person in Britain in 1941 saved 2 ounces of paper a week it would provide enough newsprint for four months – saving 16 shiploads of imported paper.

Food Facts No 100 reminisced:

> 'Today "Food Facts" reaches its century! For nearly two years this feature has helped you to solve your wartime cooking problems. Do you remember the recipes for potato pastry, wartime champ, prune roly-poly? Or the hints on making a haybox, bottling fruit without sugar, drying herbs? These are just a few of the hints and recipes which have appeared.'

As the fourth wartime Christmas approached in 1942 Woolton launched his four-point Potato Plan:

> 'Potatoes must go into action on the Food Front. You can save shipping by eating potatoes instead of bread . . . Let your patriotism direct your appetite: eat potatoes – and if you are a cook, learn new ways of serving them.'

Cooks were advised to serve potatoes for breakfast three times a week and to produce a potato dish as the main meal once a week. In 1943, as the Battle of the Atlantic against German U-boats reached its climax, the Ministry published a picture of a merchant ship sinking, with a stark message: 'THIS is the Food Fact we must never forget! Your bread costs ships. Eat home-grown potatoes instead.'

The dried egg became a staple wartime food, the Ministry stressing: 'Shell eggs are five sixths water: Why import water?'. The dried milk tin was also a basic item in the larder, since it helped supplement the limited supplies of fresh milk.

## The Radio Doctor

One of the most popular wartime broadcasters was the Radio Doctor, Charles Hill, who gave a series of practical talks, spiced with populism, entitled *Wise Eating in Wartime,* which proffered homely advice also published by the Government. Stressing the need for a varied diet, his first talk noted that 'we can't change our wives but they can change their ways, at least in giving their victims greater variety in their victuals'. The merits of fish and chips were noted:

> 'By the way, don't come over all superior at the mention of fried fish and chips. It's not only very tasty and very sweet – it's first class grub. That's true whether it's dished up with dignity to the Duke in his dining room, or scoffed by the nipper from a newspaper spread out on his knees.'

On the virtues of milk, he observed: 'A apple a day will keep no doctors away; but a pint of milk will, if it's given to children . . . That's the stuff to give 'em. Take advantage of milk while it is most plentiful.' Salad consumption was unreservedly recommended:

> 'Go all out for the cabbage leaves, the watercress and the mustard-and-cress – all of them raw. To ring the changes, go in for endive, chicory and finely grated carrot, and raw beetroot, and young dandelion, or nasturtium leaves. If you want a hot meal – well, sprinkle some pepper on it.'

In one of his BBC talks Dr Hill said that 'Britain needs more babies'. And the nation duly obliged, some 4.6 million children being born in the war years, reaching a peak of 880,000 in 1944. The welfare foods scheme, introduced in December 1941, was a morale booster since it gave extra rations for expectant mothers, including another pint of milk per day, an extra egg per allocation and an extra half ration of meat. Orange juice, cod liver oil and vitamin tablets were also available. In another radio talk, Dr Hill drew attention to one problem predator – those fathers who took more than their fair share of family food rations: 'Father needs his proper ration of meat and cheese and eggs, and no more. If he does have a little more meat, he should have less cheese and fewer eggs.'

The Ministry of Food's efforts were so successful that by 1944 expectant mothers were eating more milk and eggs per head than in peacetime and the maternal mortality rate had dropped by nearly a half.

From *When Your Baby Is Coming.*

## 1. A job worth doing

Britain needs more babies. For years the birth rate in this country went down and down and down, and if things go on as they are we are heading—and within the life-time of many alive to-day—for a big reduction in our population. True, the number of people in this country hasn't fallen yet, but the reason for that is that the death rate has been going down too. Fewer have been born, but fewer have died. But whereas the birth rate could go to nothing, there will still be a death rate for, after all, we must die some time. The death rate can't keep on going down.

In wartime, with husbands away and women on war work, one would expect the birth rate to fall, but oddly enough it now shows signs of going up. If we take the most recent figures which are available—those for last year, we find that the birth rate was the highest for any year during the last twelve years. And the number of children born dead was the lowest ever. And the number of children who died in the first year of life was equal to the lowest ever. So things are looking up. War or no war, we must see that they continue to look up.

There are many views as to why the birth rate has gone down, varying from the later age of marriage to the selfishness of young people, who are said to prefer a baby car to the real thing. Be that as it may, we want more children, and healthy and well fed children at

3

As the social historian Norman Longmate concluded:

> 'Despite bombs and rationing and war-strain, it had never been safer to have a baby, nor had a baby ever had a better chance of surviving into adult life . . . The most outstanding achievement of all was surely that at the end of six years of war the British people were far healthier than they had been at the beginning.'

Shortly after VE Day, the Ministry of Food published an advertisement stressing the need to keep up the good work:

> 'During the war the Government has made available to all children under five certain Welfare Foods which, doctors advise, are essential to health. [They] have helped to make Britain's "Blitz Babies" the bonny lot they are . . . So, mother, see that your "under five" gets these Welfare Foods every single day . . . make it a must that he has them every day from now on, no matter how healthy and rosy he looks.'

A poster drawn by Abram Games for the Army Bureau of Current Affairs in 1943 was banned following angry flak from Churchill. In order to convey the message that social progress had not been stopped by the war, it showed the Finsbury Health Centre and a child with rickets. A minute from the Prime Minister described the poster as 'a disgraceful libel on the conditions prevailing in Great Britain before the war. . . . It is a very wrong thing that the War Office should be responsible for such exaggerated and distorted propaganda.'

## Keeping Healthy

The wartime emergency meant that people had to be physically fit in order to fight, work effectively in industry, cope with air raids and endure discomforts caused by shortages. Introducing a 1943 booklet on *How to Keep Well in Wartime*, the Minister of Health, Ernest Brown, noted: '. . . as a nation we are still losing about 22 million weeks' work each year through common and often preventable illnesses.'

*The Unfit Made Fit* (1943) set out the benefits of mental and physical rehabilitation for both war and civilian casualties.

The booklet itself offered common sense advice on a whole range of health issues like proper exercise, excessive smoking and drinking, and the importance of a good diet. People were urged to continue eating wheatmeal or brown bread, the pamphlet observing: 'Russians eat black bread, and they're a tough lot.' One particular health problem singled out was the need to combat venereal disease by avoiding casual sexual intercourse: 'A hospital full of cases of gonorrhoea means loss of tanks, loss of aeroplanes, loss of guns. It also means loss of happiness, loss of health, loss of efficiency.'

A major concern of the authorities was the problem of germs spreading, symbolised by the wartime slogan on posters, 'Coughs and Sneezes Spread Diseases.' *How to Keep Well in Wartime* told people to cough or sneeze into a handkerchief and denounced any failure to do so as 'a rude and disgusting habit'. The booklet also warned about diseases like diphtheria, of which there were then 60,000 cases a year, mainly affecting children under 10: 'Inoculation against diphtheria . . . is absolutely safe and practically painless. It means little more than the prick of a needle on two occasions.'

The booklet concluded with a suitable homily: 'If you want to reach happiness, to be complete, seek health with the eagerness with which so many foolish men have sought gold. Good health is the real riches; it is up to you to get it and keep it.'

# Savings and Salvage

## Savings Campaigns

In order to finance the war and help control inflation, the gap between tax revenue and government expenditure had to be filled. Created in 1916, the National Savings movement again became a vitally important part of the Home Front.

## What Your Money Buys

THE cost of running the country is now £14,500,000 a day, of which about five-sixths is for actual war expenditure. This means that tenpence out of every shilling you pay in taxes goes to pay for victory.

The Staff of an average factory, employing 1,000 men and women workers with a total Income Tax payment of £44,000 a year, will provide £100 a day towards the cost of the war. They will pay for:

### In a day

1 large armour-piercing bomb,

*or* 3 Tommy guns,

*or* 4 depth charges,

*or* 18,000 rounds of rifle ammunition.

### In a week

1 barrage balloon,

*or* 1 heavy ambulance,

*or* 2 heavy machine-guns,

*or* 18 parachutes,

*or* 28,000 machine-gun bullets.

### In a month

1 A.A. gun,

*or* 2 anti-tank guns,

*or* 3 Bren carriers,

*or* Armament and ammunition for two harbour defence craft,

*or* 40 depth charge throwers.

### In a year

3 Valentine tanks,

*or* 4 Spitfires,

*or* 18 torpedoes,

*or* 720 small mines.

Itemising the cost of war in *The New Income Tax Quiz for Wage Earners*.

The campaign for savings began in the autumn of 1939 with the appearance of the inevitable posters. The Chancellor of the Exchequer, Sir Kingsley Wood, launched it with the slogan 'Lend to Defend the Right to be Free', a more punchy one – 'Hit Back with National Savings' – later replacing it. In early May 1940 a newspaper advertisement noted:

'Where there's a big job of work to be done it's a British instinct to "lend a hand". We can't all fight with weapons in our hands but everyone – men, women and children, too – can give direct, continuous and personal help by saving as much as they can every week and lending it to the Nation.'

Later in the summer, advertisements stressed:

'This Island Fortress faces the greatest menace in its history. Every man and woman is in the line of battle . . . To be free with your money today is not a merit. It is contemptible. To watch every penny shows your will to win . . . Lend every pound, every shilling, every penny to the Nation now.'

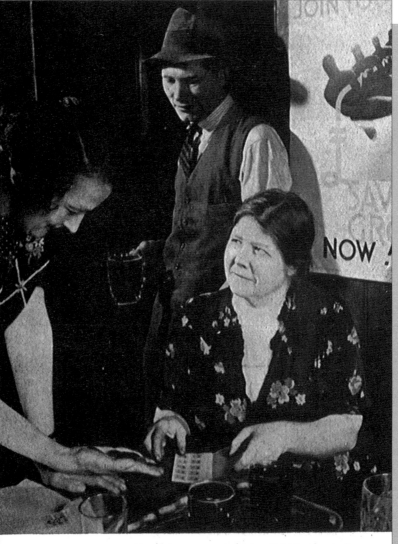

From *A People at War*.

In spite of heavy taxation the British people have already put over four thousand million pounds into National Savings. The organiser of a village savings group collects dues from a member.

47

In July 1940 an appeal was made to business leaders to invest in National War Bonds:

'The ownership or control of money is at all times a grave responsibility. In this war it is a responsibility of deeper significance. It is the imperative duty of us all to place our available money at the disposal of the State in the form in which the Government needs it and at the time when it is required.'

In July 1942 the President of the National Savings Committee stressed that battle raged ceaselessly on the Financial Front. A new slogan – 'SPEND LESS on Yourself, LEND MORE to your country' – appeared in the publicity literature, one press advertisement showing a cartoon of a grinning Hitler pinning an Iron Cross medal on a shopping basket heaped with unnecessary purchases.

Perhaps the most lasting image of wartime National Savings publicity was the Squander Bug, a large leering insect pockmarked with swastikas, which made its appearance in 1943. People were warned that the Squander Bug caused that 'fatal itch to buy for buying's sake – the symptom of shopper's disease.' Newspaper advertisements contained ditties featuring pictures of the Squander Bug:

'There was a young woman
    so loyal and true
She'd saved up her money
    and knew what to do
She simply ignored what
    the Squander Bug said
And into the Savings Bank
    put it instead.'

*Hey diddle diddle,*
*Don't finger or fiddle,*
*Those notes are a full week's pay.*
*The Squander Bug wants you to*
    *fritter the lot,*
*Keep on saving and drive him away.*

Special savings certificates could be bought, and many were given as presents to children for Christmas and birthdays. Other people agreed to regular deductions from their pay. In June 1943 nearly a quarter of the population were members of local savings groups, their efforts being encouraged by the slogan: 'Fight in the Streets. Belong to your Savings Group.' In September 1942, under the headline CABINET MEETING, a National Savings Committee advertisement said:

'No Cabinet ever met with greater determination than the Committees who plan their own Group Savings campaigns. They give their time freely and gladly because they know that money saved is a vital contribution to Victory.'

Massive publicity drives took place to encourage saving in the form of War Weapons Weeks, Warship Weeks and Wings for Victory Weeks. Morale-boosting entertainment was provided in the form of bands, flag waving military parades and sporting events. Local savings weeks backed up the national effort. If districts could raise a certain amount, they could name a tank after their town or district. Another popular way of saving money was the local Spitfire Fund, designed to raise money for an individual aircraft.

Publicity for the 1940 War Savings Week, held in June after the evacuation of Dunkirk, stressed:

'Victory now depends on speed – the speed of our planes, our ships, our mechanised armies. The speed of our factories and workers. The speed of our saving too. Start now – this week – at once – to save as you have never saved before. Every coin you put into War Savings is a bullet. Every pound part of a tank, a gun, a plane, a ship. Bring out every shilling you can spare now!'

Towards the end of the war, advertisements appeared showing civilians congratulating members of the armed forces: 'Thanks pal, for the way you're keeping Jerry on the run. We're backing you up by keeping in top gear with our War savings.' Shortly after VE Day in 1945 National Savings published an advertisement noting:

'The sunshine of a great victory plays upon our people. No enemy has trod, no enemy shall ever tread upon our soil. Let us show our gratitude by the continued saving which is needed to make this country worthy of the men and women who preserved it.'

## Salvage Drives

Massive publicity was given to the salvage drive. In July 1940 a campaign to collect scrap metal was launched in a radio broadcast by Lady Reading, head of the Women's Voluntary Service:

'I am asking for the things which you are using everyday, anything and everything, new and old, sound and broken, everything that is made of aluminium...Very few of us can be heroines on the battle-front, but we can all have the tiny thrill of thinking as we hear the news of an epic battle in the air, "Perhaps it was my saucepan that made a part of that Hurricane".'

Ministry of Supply salvage appeal advertisements jostled with those of other ministries in newspaper space and on the hoardings. During the summer of 1940 the Ministry of Supply published an advertisement: 'UP HOUSEWIVES AND AT 'EM.' It showed three women striding in tandem carrying items of salvage, accompanied by a Scottie dog with a large bone in its mouth. It appealed:

'Housewives of Britain! You have a great part to play for victory. The country urgently needs your waste paper, bones and metal. They help to make vital war supplies. You are striking a blow for your homes and your children when you save every bit of paper, bone and metal and put it out carefully. Go into action today!'

In July 1942 it was the turn of car drivers, the Ministry requesting them to hand in all their all worn out tyres and tubes.

Aluminium milk bottle tops were also a target for salvage, the Ministry pointing out that enough aluminium to build 50 Lancaster bombers was being lost each year by people throwing their bottle tops away. In 1943 the Ministry admonished: 'Is this your house? Paper, metal tins, bones, string and other materials go into it every week. But how much comes out again as salvage? Is your house slacking?'

Housewives mustn't do this. It is a punishable offence to waste food or paper ; salvage—bones, metal, paper— must be separated for easy collection.

From *A People at War.*

Local government also did its best to encourage the collection of salvage. A notice to householders issued by Cambridge Borough Council in April 1940 called on people to continue saving wastepaper and cardboard and announced that tins, rags, bottles, bones and scrap would also be collected, In addition, the notice said, 'this service will be extended to include all WASTE FOOD STUFFS and other edible material SUITABLE FOR PIG FEEDING'. A leaflet from Tottenham Borough Council pointed out that

> 'British sailors are facing the perils of German minefields and submarines to bring supplies of wood pulp, necessary for essential war material, into the country . . . No-one would ask a British seaman to endure unnecessary risks during wartime yet that is exactly what is happening so long as we waste a million tons of paper . . . DON'T WASTE PAPER AND YOU WON'T WASTE THE EFFORTS OF THE SAILORS AND MERCHANT SEAMEN.'

DATA  FOR  THE  DOUBTFUL

36,000,000 = *population over the age of* 14.

80 *per cent. of waste paper is reclaimed when repulped.*

5,000 *tons per week is the agreed consumption limit of all the British newspapers.*

*A cargo-ship of* 5,000 *tons cargo-space has been assumed.*

31

From *The Little Less.*

Early in the war advertisements appealing for binoculars appeared: 'Our Fighting Services need them all. Sell yours now. Put your pair on active service. They are wanted URGENTLY.'

Children played a major part in the drive for salvage. In May 1943 prize-winning essays on the subject were compiled in Welsh schools for HRH Princess Elizabeth, a contribution from an eight-year-old capturing the spirit of the time:

'Help! Help! Help! to beat Hitler.
Bring your pots, pans, tins, iron, paper, cardboard, rubber tyres
and all the salvage you can find
Do not waste a scrap of food or salvage.
Save Salvage Daily
Salvage is very urgent indeed and we must get more and more
Sing a song of salvage
From morning until night
Then work through all the village
And collect with all your might.

The Government took a direct hand in encouraging childrens' efforts through its Cog Scheme, the 'Cogs' being children organised by local schools as salvage collectors. Participants sang the Cog Song, 'There'll always be a Dustbin', and special Cog salvage poster competitions were organised.

In 1943 the Ministry of Supply decided to increase paper salvage from books, particularly those printed before the decline in war-time quality of paper. Book lovers were called upon to make the necessary sacrifices, the expression 'pulp fiction' becoming literally true. There was an immediate response: the public gave 56 million books, of which 5 million were passed to the armed forces and 1 million were used to replace stock lost as the result of bombing. The rest were pulped.

How to Make a Tank . . . . . . . . . . . . from an Old Bedstead

IT WOULD only be necessary for each family in the country to collect together 20 lb. of scrap iron in order to provide enough steel to build 50 new cargo ships or over 5,000 army tanks.

Practically any family could collect together from odd corners of the house, the attic or garden a number of quite useless articles made of metal—tin cans, bits of railing, old bedsteads, parts of cars and other odds and ends. These will find their way to the armament factories if left where they can be collected by the dustman (if the dustman does not take it, notify your local council). If there is a large amount, a scrap metal merchant will probably pay for it (your local police station can give the name of a nearby scrap metal merchant).

*      *      *

DATA FOR THE DOUBTFUL

12,000,000 *families in Great Britain.*

2,200 *tons of steel required to build a ship with 5,000 tons cargo space.*

*A tank of 20 tons (which is about the average weight) has been assumed as a basis of calculation.*

26      27

From *The Little Less.*

Typical of the campaign was the book drive leaflet issued by Wandsworth Borough Council in June 1943:

'500,000 BOOKS URGENTLY REQUIRED
Books wanted for:

1) THE FORCES. Those suitable for Service men and women to read.

2) BOMBED-OUT LIBRARIES. Those of rare or important value or content.

3) SALVAGE. Those not suitable for any other use.
Give your books new life.'

The salvage campaign was so successful that by 1943 three million tons of paper had been recovered and enough kitchen waste to feed over 200,000 pigs was being reclaimed each month. By the end of the war 5 million tons of scrap metal had been collected, one of the main sources being iron railings.

# Shortages

Leaving aside the impact of the Blitz and the blackout, perhaps the main feature of life for the home population was the everyday shortage or unavailability of basic commodities. From 1940 a series of Limitations of Supplies Orders were promulgated, setting out maximum amounts that could be supplied to retailers. The aim was to divert resources to arms manufacture at the cost of sacrificing many everyday comforts. The Board of Trade initiated vast publicity drives to ensure the most sensible use of existing supplies and fair shares all round.

## Make Do and Mend

In June 1941 the Government introduced clothes rationing, a measure prefaced by a broadcast from the President of the Board of Trade, Oliver Lyttelton:

> 'I know all the women will look smart, but we men may look shabby. If we do we must not be ashamed. In war the term "battle stained" is an honourable one. We must learn as civilians to be seen in clothes that are not so smart . . . When you feel tired of your old clothes remember that by making them do you are contributing some part of an aeroplane, a gun or a tank.'

The aim of the rationing scheme was to release workers for the armaments industry. The scheme was based on the points principle, each piece of clothing being given a points value.

In 1943 the Board published a Ministry of Information booklet, *Make Do and Mend*, with a foreword by its President, Hugh Dalton, who wrote: 'The Board of Trade Make Do and Mend campaign is intended to help you to get the last possible ounce of wear out of all your clothes and household things.' The slogan 'Mend and make do to save buying new' reinforced the campaign.

The booklet was designed to help 'keep clothes looking trim as long as they have to last', 'renovate children's outgrown clothes so cleverly that none is ever wasted', 'turn every scrap of good material you possess to advantage' and 'to make do with things you already have instead of buying new'. Detailed instructions were given on how to make clothes last longer and readers were informed that 'a stitch in time now saves not only extra work in the end, but precious coupons'. Hints were published on washing and ironing and advice given on how to unravel woollies and reknit them.

At least one piece of advice must have been welcomed by the vast majority of the population: 'Leave all the washing up, particularly china, to drain instead of drying it, so as to save wear on your tea towels. (But be sure to dry any tin things thoroughly and immediately).'

Another wartime character created by the publicists was Mrs Sew-and-Sew, who featured regularly in Board of Trade press advertisements. In February 1945, for instance, Mrs Sew-and-Sew advised: 'Mitts from Bits save glove coupons'. The ad continued: 'Winter mitts keep your

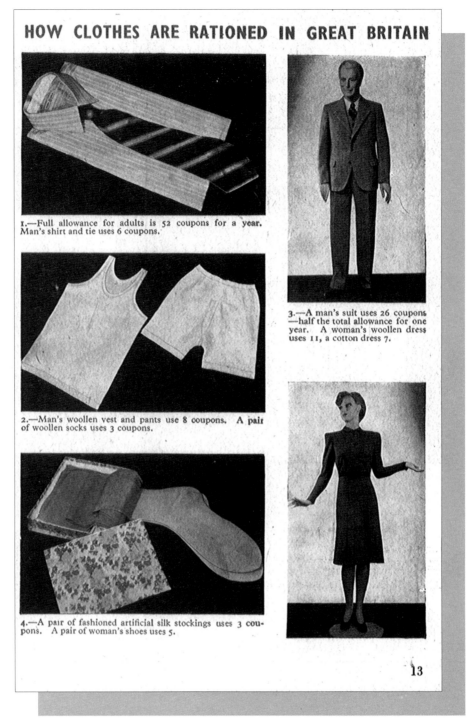

## HOW CLOTHES ARE RATIONED IN GREAT BRITAIN

1.—Full allowance for adults is 52 coupons for a year. Man's shirt and tie uses 6 coupons.

3.—A man's suit uses 26 coupons —half the total allowance for one year. A woman's woollen dress uses 11, a cotton dress 7.

2.—Man's woollen vest and pants use 8 coupons. A pair of woollen socks uses 3 coupons.

4.—A pair of fashioned artificial silk stockings uses 3 coupons. A pair of woman's shoes uses 5.

13

From *A People at War*.

hands cosy and warmer than gloves. Also they are easier to make if you follow Mrs Sew-and-Sew's directions. Why not run some up for yourself and the children.'

The Board of Trade gave special advice to pregnant women, exhorting them to avoid spending coupons on special maternity clothes:

'Almost all your existing clothes can be altered easily so that you can wear them comfortably until the baby is born, and you can wear them again afterwards. For instance, why not put an attractive matching or contrasting gathered or pleated panel in the front of the dress?'

No material must lie idle, so be a magician and turn old clothes into new. For major alterations there are many good renovation patterns on the market. Many other ideas will suggest themselves to meet special circumstances. Here are some suggestions for the home dressmaker.

## Tips to Save You Time and Trouble

1. First of all make quite sure the clothes cannot be worn as they are, with perhaps a little darning or patching. Don't waste precious time just for the sake of making something new and different.

2. If you decide that the garment is quite unwearable, unpick it completely and with patience in order to salvage every inch of material; then wash it or send it to the cleaners. If the material is faded or patchy have it dyed a darker colour.

3. Remember the material has already seen some years of use, so treat it gently.

4. If you particularly like any part of the garment such as the sleeves or neckline, make a paper pattern of it for future use.

5. Before cutting out the new gar-ment hold the material up to the light and note any thin places or holes. Tack round them with contrasting coloured thread so that you can avoid them when laying out the pattern.

6. Unless you are an expert never attempt to cut out without using a pattern.

7. When you choose a pattern be sure the size conforms to your *up-to-date* measurements.

8. Measure yourself or the child for whom you are making something new to make quite sure the pattern will fit; don't just chance it.

9. Don't cut down grown-up's clothes to make clothes for the children, which they don't really need, just for the sake of making something new for them.

From *Make Do and Mend*.

Once the baby was born, the Board told mothers, 'babies don't need nearly as many clothes as people used to think.' Rubber knickers were not necessary and 'napkins, put on properly, can look very neat and the external layer is inclined to overheat'. A set of clothing for babies could include four or five gowns, four vests, three matinee jackets, three pairs of bootees and two medium sized shawls. As for cots, 'a laundry basket or even a deep drawer, suitably lined, can be adapted to make a very useful cot for the first few months'.

# Cutting Fuel Consumption

Although petrol was rationed, many of the Government's parliamentary supporters were opposed to the rationing of gas and electricity, so this was never imposed. Instead, a long publicity campaign was launched in the summer of June 1942, with a series of advertisements and posters exhorting the population to cut fuel consumption. Under the slogan LESS LIGHT – MORE GUNS the Ministry of Fuel and Power said: 'If all of us halved our lighting, the saving would mean hundreds of thousands of tons of coal for vital war production. Start tonight.' The dripping tap was singled out for particular criticism: 'Never waste any water, hot or cold. Turn all taps right off.' Those seeking comfort in a hot bath were warned:

> 'Do you know that if we put 3 inches less water in our bath, many thousands of tons of coal will be saved for war production in a year? Never have more than 5 inches of water in your bath. See what you can do about it . . . Release MORE COAL for the WAR DRIVE'.

Newspaper advertisements, 1943.

The need to save gas was emphasised:

> 'Never allow flames to lick the sides of a kettle or saucepan – the water won't boil any quicker and it wastes gas...Cut down hot meals to a minimum, and go easy with the geyser.'

In huge press advertisements consumers were urged to work out their own target for fuel consumption:

> 'Here are YOUR battle orders . . . Keep within your target by doing with less fuel and we shall win the Battle for Fuel. Watch your fuel consumption day by day and week by week to make sure you are keeping inside the target . . . We will work together and show that a free people can freely make the sacrifices necessary for victory.'

The targets consisted of fuel units, one unit equalling a gallon of paraffin, 50 units of electricity, 500 cubic feet of gas or half a hundredweight of coal.

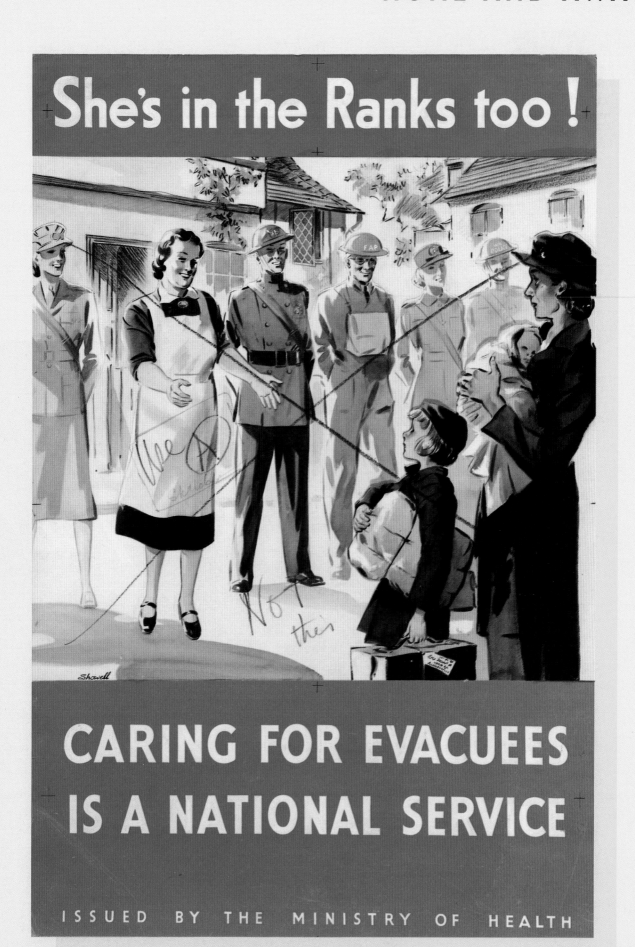

One poster that never saw the light of day – no doubt because it might have deterred the mothers of potential evacuees from handing them over.

The 17,500 excursion trains that ran in peacetime were all cancelled to make way for freight and troop trains. Taking to the car was not an option: petrol was not available for 'pleasure motoring'.

The difficulties of travelling in the blackout were compounded by the removal of station names.

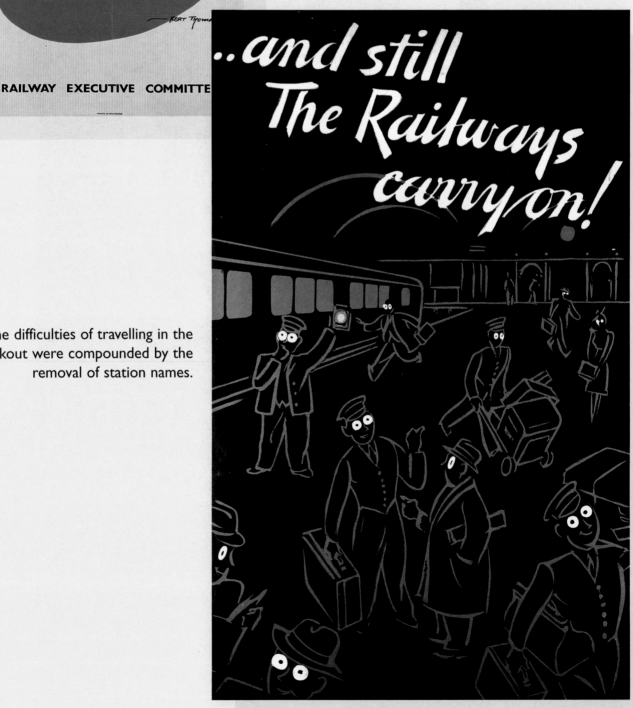

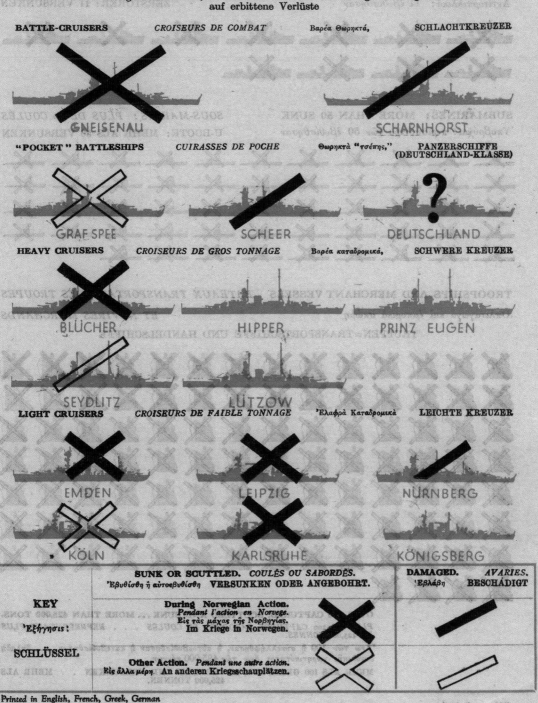

Lightweight leaflet for dropping over mainland Europe, dated April 1940. The information on it was slightly optimistic.

# STAMPING OUT THE U-BOATS !

**1** Detection instruments on a British destroyer gave warning of the approach of a German submarine. Instantly, the destroyer began to circle the area at top speed. As she went, depth-charges were fired overside. A ring of violent under-water explosions hemmed in the doomed and hidden U-boat. Within a few minutes, as the deadly depth-charges closed in upon her, she got the force of one of the explosions. Her plates were wrenched and began to open as the rivets came loose. Her German commander's one thought was to get back to the surface. Up she came, in a smother of foam . . .

**2** . . . The moment the submarine's conning-tower breaks the surface of the sea, as her ballast tanks empty and she bobs to the top, the hatches are opened and the Germans start to jump into the water, like peas bursting from a pod. They have given up all hope of attacking the convoy, now : they have forgotten their Führer's screaming boasts : they are just Germans, scrambling for safety, who have realised what British sea-power really means . . .

**3** . . . Now they are all in the water, all except one, for they know that the British, true to the ancient traditions of humanity at sea—traditions which only pirates ignore—will put a boat into the water and save as many of them as possible. The U-boat is settling down as the sea floods her, seeping through her opened plates . . .

**4** . . . Last man aboard, hesitating to the last minute, waits until the destroyer's boat draws near before jumping over the side . . .

**5** . . . The U-boat's death-plunge. All in a matter of minutes the grim scene is ended—just one of the scores of German U-boats which sailed out to attack shipping, and never went back.

BY DEPTH-CHARGE, BOMB, AND SHELL-FIRE, Britain's Royal Navy and Royal Air Force bring swift and sudden death to German submarines. Daily they are driven from the shipping routes. Not all of Hitler's U-boats are out at one time— they must spend days in harbour. There, they are sunk and smashed by frequent visits of British bombers, giving their crews a taste of what is waiting for them when they sail. Out at sea, they are watched for and found by patrolling aircraft, and then there is no escape—not even by hiding motionless, on the sea-bottom. Sooner or later they are bombed, depth-charged, sunk by a destroyer's guns.

But Britain does not give the tally of submarines she has sunk. Britain knows the terror which eats into the hearts of German submarine crews as they see British bombs blasting German docks. Those crews know that when they disappear, no one will ever hear about it. They know that hundreds of their comrades have gone out—never to return. And the Germans would very much like to hear where and when their U-boats were lost. So the British Admiralty keeps its own counsel—British bombs, shells, and depth-charges are the best reply to Goebbels !

## BRITAIN IS SINKING GERMAN U-BOATS AS FAST AS GERMANY IS PUTTING THEM OUT TO SEA!

Printed in England by Fosh & Cross Ltd., London                    August, 1941

Drama on the high seas in a leaflet published in August 1941.

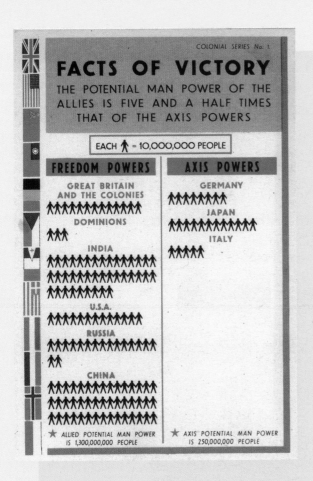

**COLONIAL SERIES No. 1.**

# FACTS OF VICTORY
## THE POTENTIAL MAN POWER OF THE ALLIES IS FIVE AND A HALF TIMES THAT OF THE AXIS POWERS

EACH 🚶 = 10,000,000 PEOPLE

| FREEDOM POWERS | AXIS POWERS |
|---|---|
| GREAT BRITAIN AND THE COLONIES | GERMANY |
| DOMINIONS | JAPAN |
| INDIA | ITALY |
| U.S.A. | |
| RUSSIA | |
| CHINA | |

★ ALLIED POTENTIAL MAN POWER IS 1,300,000,000 PEOPLE  ★ AXIS POTENTIAL MAN POWER IS 250,000,000 PEOPLE

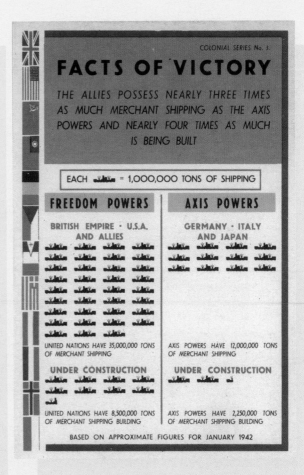

**COLONIAL SERIES No. 3.**

# FACTS OF VICTORY
## THE ALLIES POSSESS NEARLY THREE TIMES AS MUCH MERCHANT SHIPPING AS THE AXIS POWERS AND NEARLY FOUR TIMES AS MUCH IS BEING BUILT

EACH 🚢 = 1,000,000 TONS OF SHIPPING

| FREEDOM POWERS | AXIS POWERS |
|---|---|
| BRITISH EMPIRE · U.S.A. AND ALLIES | GERMANY · ITALY AND JAPAN |

UNITED NATIONS HAVE 35,000,000 TONS OF MERCHANT SHIPPING | AXIS POWERS HAVE 12,000,000 TONS OF MERCHANT SHIPPING

**UNDER CONSTRUCTION** | **UNDER CONSTRUCTION**

UNITED NATIONS HAVE 8,500,000 TONS OF MERCHANT SHIPPING BUILDING | AXIS POWERS HAVE 2,250,000 TONS OF MERCHANT SHIPPING BUILDING

BASED ON APPROXIMATE FIGURES FOR JANUARY 1942

HOW THE **R.A.F.** IS SINKING AXIS SHIPPING

1941
MAY DECEMBER
**610** SHIPS
SUNK OR DAMAGED

1940
MAY DECEMBER
**110** SHIPS
SUNK OR DAMAGED

BRITAIN'S AIR OFFENSIVE GROWS!

**BRITISH FIGHTERS CLEAR THE SKIES OF GERMAN BOMBERS**

"We shall do everything in our power to crush Hitler"
F. D. Roosevelt, President of the United States.

Inspirational posters of battleships were supplemented with the handy 'pocket facts' approach of postcards. Stickers (bottom right) were often dropped over occupied countries to be stuck in public places as a mark of defiance against German occupying forces.

# THE BRITISH EMPIRE'S
# KING and QUEEN

In their garden at Windsor, the Princesses dig, hoe, trim paths, weed, and cart and carry all their produce.

Princess Margaret Rose.

Princess Elizabeth.

It was not only the home front that had to be rallied; the colonies, as a rich source of raw materials and labour, had to be addressed: 'Wherever else did human idealism and practical sense combine to weld one-fourth of the human race, scattered over a quarter of this globe, into an entity based on respect for individual freedom, and spontaneously generating the willing service of all in the common interest?'
(*The British Empire's King and Queen*)

10

# Petroleum Products from TRINIDAD

## FOR FUELLING SHIPS

Trinidad has a famous natural pitch lake, as well as large oilfields, and is the greatest producer of mineral oil in the Colonial Empire at present. In these days of mechanized warfare and constant sea patrols, petroleum products are essential for fuelling 'planes, tanks, lorries and ships. A lack of petroleum in a war of machines could have a disastrous effect on the country who lacked it.

# Sea Island Cotton from the WINDWARD ISLANDS
### (LEEWARD ISLANDS AND BARBADOS)

## FOR BARRAGE BALLOONS

Wonderful rugged scenery and luxurious vegetation are typical features of the Windward and Leeward Islands and Barbados, and part of the luxurious vegetation is Sea Island Cotton. This cotton makes a beautiful material that has the texture of silk. Popular before the war for luxury shirts, it plays a great part in the defence of Britain to-day in making barrage balloons to protect cities from enemy dive-bombers.

# Rubber from CEYLON

## MAKES TYRES
## FOR ARMY VEHICLES

Although Ceylon is always associated with tea, the cultivation of rubber is nearly as extensive and even more important. With the Axis in control of so many rubber plantations in the Far East, the increasing supply from Ceylon is vital. Rubber is used for army vehicles' tyres and also for rubber dinghies, to save the lives of pilots who bale out of their aircraft over the sea.

*Colonial Products Make Frontline Weapons* showed the people of the colonies the ultimate destination of the fruits of their labour, whether in mines and cotton fields, on sheep farms or elsewhere.

VICTORY IS VITAL!

GERMANS WOULD ROB
WEST AFRICANS OF THEIR PRODUCE

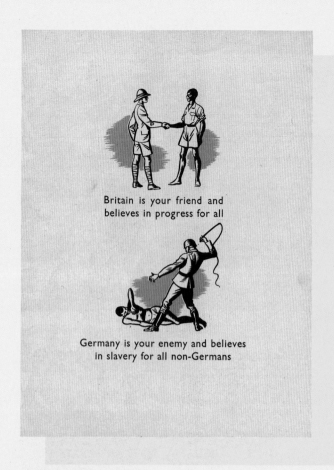

Britain is your friend and
believes in progress for all

Germany is your enemy and believes
in slavery for all non-Germans

*Building in war time is waste of raw materials*

AND THIS IS WHY...

*Timber, metal, bricks and cement
can all play a more useful part
in the war effort than that of
making new houses. The Allied armies
need these materials to build
temporary quarters for their troops.
Timber is needed in the shipyards,
metal is required for armaments,
bricks and cement are wanted for
air raid shelters and defence posts.*

*Use local materials for essential repairs*

10

11

'People in Britain and other parts of the British Empire are doing without
many of the things they had in peace time, for only in this way can Victory
be won. We in Africa must also do without many things, for the war is a
period of sacrifice by all for Victory'. From *Working Together for Victory*,
a leaflet aimed at West Africa.

In the autumn of 1942 and the winter of 1943 the Ministry of Fuel and Power intensified its publicity effort through a series of Battle for Fuel Communiqués. The first stressed that fuel reserves were needed 'for the time of crisis when our enemy the Winter assaults us on the wings of an East Wind escorted by Jack Frost'. The sixth said that the resolute and determined fuel saver could save ammunition in the grate and thereby help shoot down one Messerschmidt or one night bomber.

In October 1942 the population was urged to share their fires with their neighbours so that they could sit in one well-warmed room: 'Some people say this means a change in our national habits. What if it does? We are all in this war together.' And another message was rammed home:

'CINDERS COUNT! When your fires are going, don't forget to sieve the cinders. If all the cinders in Great Britain in open fires in one year were sieved, no less than 2,000,000 tons of coal would be saved.'

And one more:

'KEEP THE POKER ON THE HEARTH. A good sized lump of coal weighs about 5 lb. Broken up into five pieces, it will blaze away fiercely. Left whole and well banked it will burn for nearly three times as long . . . So go easy with the poker.'

The cold suffered by the Russian people was invoked in 1943: 'Every ounce of fuel saved by you helps to make more tanks, guns, planes and shells for our Russian allies.'

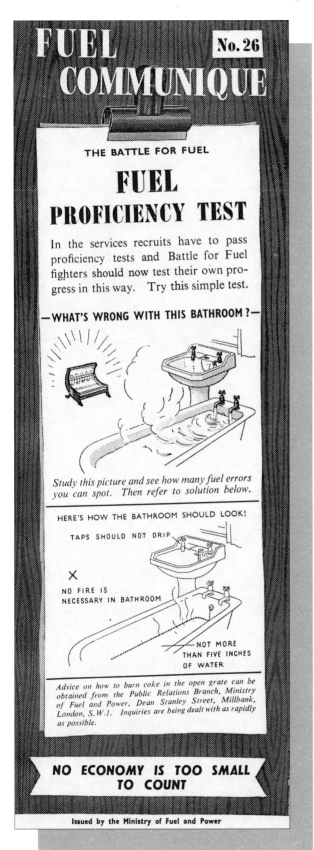

FUEL COMMUNIQUE No. 26

THE BATTLE FOR FUEL

## FUEL PROFICIENCY TEST

In the services recruits have to pass proficiency tests and Battle for Fuel fighters should now test their own progress in this way. Try this simple test.

— WHAT'S WRONG WITH THIS BATHROOM ? —

*Study this picture and see how many fuel errors you can spot. Then refer to solution below.*

HERE'S HOW THE BATHROOM SHOULD LOOK!

TAPS SHOULD NOT DRIP

✗ NO FIRE IS NECESSARY IN BATHROOM

NOT MORE THAN FIVE INCHES OF WATER

*Advice on how to burn coke in the open grate can be obtained from the Public Relations Branch, Ministry of Fuel and Power, Dean Stanley Street, Millbank, London, S.W.1. Inquiries are being dealt with as rapidly as possible.*

**NO ECONOMY IS TOO SMALL TO COUNT**

Issued by the Ministry of Fuel and Power

An advertisement urging readers to save fuel pays tribute to the stoicism of the Russians.

## Is Your Journey Really Necessary?

In 1943 a poster placarded on railway stations and other sites said: 'The time has come for every person to search his conscience before making a railway journey. It is more than ever vital to ask yourself "Is my journey really necessary?"' Space was needed for special military trains, particularly in the build-up to the D-Day landings in 1944, and facilities for ordinary travellers had to be cut back in the interests of the war effort. In May 1942 the Government directed the withdrawal of almost all restaurant cars to make additional space for passengers, who were also asked to bring their own cups to station refreshment buffets. Nevertheless, first class travel was still permitted with the exception of trains in the London transport area.

In July 1942 the Ministry of Information 'What Do I Do?' series touched on the question of holiday travel:

> 'As the railways are busy with war traffic I do not travel far from home but make the most of my holiday in my own district, taking advantage of local arrangements. And wherever I go among strangers, I do not gossip about my war work.'

The four railway companies – GWR, LMS, LNER and SR – published press advertisements pointing out that 'IF 50 PEOPLE DON'T TRAVEL, 1 TANK CAN', concluding with the ditty:

> 'At this most important time
> Needless travel is a "crime"'

**SEASIDE HOLIDAYS** *are just a pleasant memory now*

A British family spends a holiday sight-seeing in the art galleries and museums of their own town instead of picnicking on the sands at the seaside.

57

From *A People at War*.

Another advertisement in 1942 pointed out that 'WAR SUPPLIES are urgently needed on all Allied fronts. They must have priority. DON'T TRAVEL unless it is absolutely necessary.' The Christmas break in 1942 provided no let up, as a railways advertisement made plain: 'The Minister of War Transport directs that no more passenger trains are to be run between 21 and 29 December, inclusive, than on any ordinary day in December. The public is warned that if more people seek to travel than can be accommodated, they will find themselves stranded.'

Wartime travel was, of course, affected by the blackout and the removal of station signs, a step taken to help confuse an enemy invasion. One poster advised: 'If you can't see the name and can't hear the porter's voice – ask another traveller . . . If you know where you are by local signs and sounds, please tell others in the carriage.' Another problem was air raids, and special advice was drawn up:

'If an air raid occurs while you are in the train

1) Do not attempt to leave the train if it stops away from a station, unless requested by the guard to do so. You are safer where you are.

2) Pull the blinds down, both by day and night, as a protection against flying glass.

3) If room is available, lie down on the floor.'

Long distance coach and bus travel was severely affected by the shortage of fuel and of rubber for tyres. In October 1942 the bus companies announced the suspension of these services, noting: 'The discomfort and inconvenience are very much regretted, but these the public are asked to accept as a contribution to the war effort.'

In 1942 queuing for buses became compulsory. Publicity films were used to back up this regulation by slamming anti-social behaviour, one showing a portly man called George getting on the bus and alighting at the next stop, much to the fury of other passengers. The film was accompanied by the following soundtrack:

'You'll wonder why we make a fuss,
If George decides to take a bus,
But look again and you will see,
That George ain't all that George should be,
He's only got a step to go,
A couple of hundred yards or so,
While others further down the queue,
Have far to go and lots to do.

'When George gets on we often find,
That other folk get left behind,
He pays his fare and rides a stage,
Then off he pops – and see the rage,
And seeing this gives George a jog,
"Perhaps I'm just a transport hog". '

Such admonishments could be and were backed up by fines levied on offenders jumping the queue.

Petrol rationing started at the beginning of the war, the ration allowing enough petrol for about 100–200 miles a month. In order to provide fuel for bombers and fighters, cuts in the ration continued to take place, and in March 1942 the Government took the plunge by refusing to allow motorists to have their basic ration. Another aim was to end pleasure motoring, which had given rise to much public anger, and to keep all unessential cars off the road.

(Above) A familiar sight on every main road in Britain during a peace-time weekend.

(Below) The same road to-day. The only cars allowed on the road are used for essential war work. No petrol is obtainable for pleasure motoring.

From *A People at War*

# Arts and entertainment

Important efforts were made by the Government to keep up morale through entertainment, the BBC taking its full part. People sought release from the strains imposed by war work, the daily struggle with shortages and the perils faced by soldiers and civilians.

## The BBC

One of the most popular BBC programmes, backed by Minister of Labour Bevin, was *Workers' Playtime*, which was broadcast from war factories; by the end of the war there were three transmissions a week. Traditional music hall shows were popular, as were American radio variety programmes. Dance music was regularly performed by artists like Henry Hall, Billy Cotton and Victor Sylvester. The most popular comedy show during the war was Tommy Handley's *ITMA*

Reference..................................................................................

TO:    Mr. Francis Williams

FROM:  Admiral Thomson

Re the attached.

I have never at any time been impressed with the value of switch censoring, but in any event I feel we might dispense with it, after the German war is over, in the case of variety programmes and non-news talks. The type of danger which arises at present, due to Tommy Handley or Will Fyffe interpolating their own gags, is hardly likely to exist in the Japanese war, e.g. "I wish the plumber would come and mend my frozen pipes", which is a stop now, would be harmless in the Japanese war. On the other hand, I cannot anticipate Tommy Handley suddenly saying "2 battleships are leaving for the Far East tomorrow".

In that connection, the scripts of all programmes will, as now, be precensored.

*G.P.T.*

24th October, 1944.

Comics caused headaches for censors then as now, but for different reasons. (Minute from the MOI's Chief Press Censor to the Director of Press and Publications)

(*It's That Man Again*) which poked fun at officialdom and created amusement out of topical wartime situations; supporting characters included the German spy Funf, the heavy drinking Colonel Chinstrap and the charlady Mrs Mopp.

The BBC acted as a major cultural impresario by commissioning works from composers and authors, employing actors and musicians and publishing talks and poetry in its weekly *Listener* magazine.

The BBC also met the demand for information and discussion about the course of the war and current social and political issues. The nine o'clock news in the evening became a national institution and was followed by short talks, *Postscripts*, featuring speakers such as J.B. Priestley, some of whose talks did not go down well with Churchill and some other ministers on the grounds that they were too left wing. Other *Postscripts* speakers included A.P. Herbert. By the middle of the war about a third of the population was tuning into the *Brains Trust* programme, featuring a panel of speakers including the academic philosopher Professor Joad and the scientist Julian Huxley.

## ENSA

On the outbreak of war the Entertainments National Service Association (ENSA) was created to provide entertainment for troops and for civilian workers in factories. Concerts were laid on in factories, cathedrals and large halls, the main symphony orchestras taking part in nearly 400 concerts for war workers. The demand for lighter entertainment was also met by ENSA, comedians enjoying ample scope for their talents.

## CEMA

The provision of serious music and drama was the main purpose of the Council for the Encouragement of Music and Drama (CEMA); grants

Audience at a National Gallery Concert

The National Gallery lunchtime concerts were immensely popular, as this photograph from *Music* (in the 'Britain Advances' series) shows.

were provided by the Treasury. Musicians toured the country, playing in small villages and towns and during lunch breaks at factories. In addition, hundreds of symphony concerts were backed and opera and ballet brought to audiences for whom they were a new experience. Weekday lunch-time concerts in the National Gallery, performed by artists such as Myra Hess, Ida Haendel, Peter Pears and Kathleen Ferrier, provided solace for Londoners. In addition, CEMA organised tours of exhibitions under the title Art for the People.

## Current Affairs

There was also a demand for information on the war and for books on politics and current affairs. The Government's Stationery Office had a number of bestsellers, including the Beveridge Report on social security (over 600,000 copies sold) and well-produced illustrated books on topics like the Blitz, Bomber Command, Fighter Command and anti-aircraft defence. Allen Lane's series of Penguin Specials covered every conceivable wartime current affairs topic ranging from books about map reading and signalling for the Home Guard to the need for a national health service.

## Army Bureau for Current Affairs

During the war the Army, too, was involved in adult education for the forces. The Army Bureau for Current Affairs, formed in June 1941, gave soldiers the opportunity to discuss current affairs and had its own theatre group which put on drama-documentaries. Its local agents were the officers of the Army Educational Corps. One booklet, *Education in the British Army*, published in 1944, emphasised the need for freedom of discussion during classes: 'The soldier may ask any and every question. He can talk, instead of being talked to. He can argue, and express his doubts or misgivings. He is a citizen as well as a soldier, a thinking individual and not a mere number in a regimental list.'

## War Artists Advisory Committee

When war broke out the Government set up the War Artists Advisory Committee, which commissioned paintings on wartime themes on behalf of the Ministry of Information. These were exhibited in the National Gallery to replace old masters which had been transferred to a safer place. Graham Sutherland was commissioned to paint pictures of mines and factories, while Stanley Spencer produced a series of nine large paintings of ships being built in a Clydeside yard. Over a hundred artists painted for the Committee, some of them full time.

Introducing the first catalogue of official war pictures circulated by the Ministry, Eric Newton wrote that the artist had found a subject and an employer: 'And after years in vain waiting for commissions, at last he is commanded to paint by the State . . . He is no longer a man playing games with a paint-box for his own amusement. He is an employed workman. And that is good for him. It gives him a purpose and it gives his work guts.'

# WAR PICTURES BY BRITISH ARTISTS

*by Eric Newton*

In a hundred years' time, when this war that now fills so much of our daily lives and thoughts has become a matter for history books and legend, how will our descendants know what it felt like to live through the dark days and wild nights of 1941 ? History books will give them the bare facts, stories handed down from father to son will add a little detailed embroidery, but how is the fantastic truth that lies beneath the war's surface to be told ? To what contemporary records will the unborn generations turn in their attempts to get at that truth ?

The files of our daily newspapers will certainly offer them a glimpse, but a distorted glimpse, full of infuriating gaps and bewildering contradictions. Photographs will add a little visual information, but how flavourless and how tantalisingly incomplete it will be. The newspapers will record the numbers of prisoners taken and the names of the towns captured, the questions asked in Parliament and the amount of butter consumable per head per week. The photographs will show the shape of a Spitfire or the outward aspect of a house destroyed by bombs ; but who is to hand on to future generations the tension and the excitement, the weariness and the laughter, the speed and the power of to-day's war ?

From the introduction to the catalogue of the first exhibition of War Pictures by British Artists.

From the second
exhibition of War
Pictures by British
Artists.

L. DUFFY
*Aftermath*

From
the third
exhibition
of War
Pictures
by British
Artists.

EDWARD ARDIZZONE
*Storming an Enemy Post*

Gp/47/19.

August 1st, 1940.

Dear Dame Laura,

I am writing to you at the request of the
Artists' Advisory Committee which is, as I expect
you know, responsible for making recommendations
for the appointment of artists to paint war records of all kinds.

The Committee hope that you will accept a
commission to paint the portrait of Acting Section
Officer Pearson, of the W.A.A.F., who has recently
been decorated for bravery.

The Committee have found that wellknown
artists who are accustomed to receive large fees
have been good enough to carry out work on their
behalf for considerably lower fees than they would
normally expect to receive, both as a matter of
National Service and because by so doing more money
than would otherwise be available is left over for
commissioning other artists. We very much hope that
you will be prepared to paint this portrait for a
fee of 35 guineas. We can, in addition, defray any
travelling expenses which may be necessary and pay
a maintenance allowance at the rate of one pound a
day should you require to be away from home.

I very much hope that you will accept this
commission. As soon as I have heard that you are
willing to do so, I shall ask the finance people to
send you a copy of the usual contract letter and
shall put you in touch with the Ministry of Home
Security who will make the necessary arrangements
for sittings.

Yours sincerely,

E. M. O'R. DICKEY

Dame Laura Knight's portrait of Acting Section Officer Pearson, the first woman to be awarded the
George Cross, appeared in the third exhibition of War Pictures by British Artists.

# A better world?

The question of war aims and social reform in post-war Britain gave rise to considerable discussion among the people and, of course, to different opinions among politicians in Churchill's coalition government. In the minds of the people there was a clear link between morale and a better post-war world, since the war touched everybody in their daily lives, whether as soldiers, civilian industrial workers, housewives or farm labourers. There was a widespread feeling that the massive sacrifices being made should not mean a return to the mass unemployment of pre-war days and that reforms of the existing health, education, housing and social security systems were essential. Once the country's survival was no longer in question, these issues became more prominent, as was shown by the attention given to the recommendations of the Beveridge Report in December 1942.

In 1940 and 1941 the main war aim was to mobilise the war economy, and post-war reconstruction was placed on the back-burner. Home Intelligence reports, however, consistently recorded criticisms of the better off, as one noted in May 1941: 'There is growing evidence of a feeling among certain sections of the public that "everything is not fair and equal and that therefore our sacrifices are not worthwhile".' In particular, the report said that there was some belief that the rich were less hit by rationing on the grounds that they could afford to eat at expensive restaurants, could afford high priced goods in short demand,

It is a gigantic and exciting task—this re-building of the homes of a nation. It will absorb the labour, the skill, and the energy of hundreds of thousands of people—not only the skilled workers of the building industry, but many who have been engaged in the great war industries

House made in a factory

soon to be switched over to the more constructive tasks of peace. New methods, new materials will be employed. Factories will turn out whole sections of houses delivered ready-built to the sites where they will be speedily erected. The Government has decided upon a new "full employment" policy for everyone; the new housing programme, tackled with energy and enthusiasm, should go far to make that realizable in the first ten years after the war.

From *Houses That Are Homes*, a 1945 publication in the 'Britain Advances' series spend more on clothes and receive preferential treatment in shops. This did not mean that there was a yearning for revolutionary upheaval, as another Home Intelligence report made plain in 1942: 'It seems clear that "people are willing to bear any sacrifice, if a 100 per cent effort can be reached, and the burden fairly borne by all".'

This mood accounted for the extraordinary reception given by the people to the Beveridge Report, which recommended the inclusion of everyone in a reorganised social insurance system and the creation of a national health service. The reaction of the Government publicists was confused. Although the Ministry of Information issued a summary of the report and the BBC broadcast details in 22 languages, the War Office withdrew an Army Bureau of Current Affairs pamphlet giving details of the plan. Differences were expressed among Cabinet ministers. In January 1943 Churchill issued a Cabinet memorandum expressing concern about the danger of expectations being raised too high: 'It is for this reason of not wishing to deceive the people by false hopes . . . that I have refrained so far from making promises about the future.' The Deputy Prime Minister, Clement Attlee, expressed concern about the preparation of mere paper schemes: '. . . unless the Government is prepared to be as courageous in planning for peace as it has been in carrying on the war, there is extreme danger of disaster when the war ends.'

During the Commons debate on the Beveridge proposals in February 1942, the Government said that, while there could not be any binding commitment to introduce legislation during the war, it favoured the scheme in principle.

As the war neared its end the Government's Reconstruction Committee approved the Beveridge plan in White Papers on a national health service, social insurance, insurance against industrial injuries, and employment policy. Introduced in 1944, the employment document undertook to 'secure a balanced industrial development' in high unemployment areas and to 'accept in future the responsibility for taking action at the earliest possible opportunity to arrest a threatened slump'. Legislation was also passed providing for the payment of family allowances for children and R.A. Butler's 1944 Education Act made provision for free secondary education for all in England and Wales. Similar legislation for Scotland was passed in 1945. In addition, the wartime coalition published proposals on town and country planning.

The main elements of the post-war welfare state were, therefore, in place ready for implementation and improvement when peace broke out in 1945 and Churchill's national coalition was replaced by the Attlee Government after the July general election.

# Further reading

The following books were particularly useful in the preparation of the text.

Addison, Paul. *The Road to 1945*. Pimlico, 1994.

————*Churchill on the Home Front 1900–1955*. Pimlico, 1993.

Balfour, Michael. *Propaganda in War 1939–1945: Organisations, Policies and Publics in Britain and Germany*. Routledge & Kegan Paul, 1979.

Bliss Jr, Edward. *The Broadcasts of Edward R. Murrow 1938-1961*. Macmillan, 1968.

Bramsted, Ernest K. *Goebbels and National Socialist Propaganda 1925-1945*. The Cresset Press, 1965.

Briggs, Asa. *The History of Broadcasting in the United Kingdom*. Volume III: *The War of Words*. Oxford University Press, 1970.

Bullock, Alan. *The Life and Times of Ernest Bevin*. Vol II: *Minister of Labour 1940–1945*. Heinemann, 1967.

Calder, Angus. *The People's War*. Pimlico, 1992.

————*The Myth of the Blitz*. Pimlico, 1992.

Churchill, Winston. *Into Battle*. Cassell, 1941.

Cruikshank, Charles. *The Fourth Arm: Psychological Warfare 1938–1945*. Oxford University Press, 1981.

Donoughue, Bernard and Jones, G.W. *Herbert Morrison: Portrait of a Politician*. Weidenfeld & Nicholson, 1973.

Gilbert, Martin. *Finest Hour: Winston S. Churchill 1939–41*. Minerva, 1989.

Harris, Kenneth. *Attlee*. Weidenfeld & Nicholson, 1984

Harrison, Tom. *Living Through the Blitz*. Penguin, 1978.

Hewison, Robert. *Under Siege: Literary Life in London 1939–45*. Quartet Books, 1979.

King, Francis and Matthews, George. *About Turn: The British Communist Party and the War. The Verbatim Record of the Central Committee Meetings of 25 September and 2–3 October 1939*. Lawrence & Wishart, 1990.

Longmate, Norman. *How We Lived Then*. Arrow Books, 1977.

Mass Observation. *War Begins at Home*. Chatto and Windus, 1940.

McLaine, Ian. *Ministry of Morale: Home Front Morale and the Ministry of Information in World War II*. Allen & Unwin, 1979.

Munton, Alan. *English Fiction of the Second World War*. Faber & Faber, 1989.

Nicolson, Nigel (ed.). *Harold Nicolson: Diaries and Letters 1939–1945*. Fontana Books, 1970.

Priestley, J.B. *Postscripts*. Heinemann, 1940.

Selwyn, Francis. *Hitler's Englishman: The Crime of Lord Haw-Haw*. Penguin, 1993.

Sperber, A.M. *Murrow: His Life and Times*. Michael Joseph, 1987.

Williams, Francis. *Press, Parliament and People*. Heinemann, 1946.

Yass, Marion. *This is Your War: Home Front Propaganda in the Second World War*. HMSO, 1983.

Printed in the U.K. for HMSO Dd 300922 C50 5/95 13110